Good Ideas

for Creating a More Ethical and Effective Workplace

JOSEPH & EDNA
JOSEPHSON
INSTITUTE
OF ETHICS

By

Steven R. Nish

Senior Editor

Josephson Institute of Ethics

A production of the Department of Publications and
Communications at the Josephson Institute of Ethics

Wes Hanson
VP/ Department Director

Steven R. Nish
Senior Editor / Webmaster

Dan McNeill
Editor

Melissa Mertz
Instructional Designer

Andrew Acalinovich
Art Director

Peter Chen
Assistant Editor / Graphics

Unlimited Publishing
Bloomington, Indiana

Josephson Institute of Ethics
Los Angeles, California

Distributing Publisher
Unlimited Publishing LLC
Bloomington, Indiana
www.unlimitedpublishing.com

Contributing Publisher
Josephson Institute of Ethics
Los Angeles, California
www.josephsoninstitute.org

UNLIMITED
PUBLISHING

JOSEPH & EDNA
JOSEPHSON
INSTITUTE
OF ETHICS

Unlimited Publishing LLC ("UP") provides worldwide book design, production, marketing, and distribution services for professional authors and publishers, serving as distributing publisher. Sole responsibility for the content of each work rests with the author(s) and/or contributing publisher(s). Information or opinions expressed herein may not be interpreted in any way as originating from or endorsed by UP, or any of its officers, employees, agents, or assigns.

The book design makes use of one or more typefaces specifically licensed by and customized for the exclusive use of Unlimited Publishing.

Cover Design: Andrew Acalinovich

First Edition

Copies of this fine book and many others are available to order at:
www.charactercounts.org and
www.unlimitedpublishing.com/authors

ISBN 1-58832-135-5

Library of Congress Control Number: 2005927654

Unlimited Publishing
Bloomington, Indiana

Josephson Institute of Ethics
Los Angeles, California

Good Ideas
for Creating a More Ethical and Effective Workplace

TABLE OF CONTENTS

Introduction 1

The Six Pillars of Character 4

Part 1: Good Ideas for Creating an Ethical Workplace

Open Communication
Keep Employees Informed 7
Encourage Candid Employee Feedback 8
Clarify the Code of Conduct 9
Offer Hotlines for Ethical Guidance or Whistleblowing 10

Audits
Issue Corporate Accountability Reports 11
Conduct Social and Environmental Responsibility Audits 13
Use Core Ethical Values as Audit Criteria 15

Accounting
Manage With an Open Book 16

Ethics in Hiring and Firing
Issue Guidelines to Recruiters and Interviewers 17
Show Respect and Sensitivity in Terminations 19

Employee Relations
Manage Diversity Effectively 20
Guarantee Fair Treatment 21
Promote Tolerance 22

Employee Recognition
Give Awards for Employee Excellence 23
Tell the Company's Story 24

Employee Ideas
Take Employee Suggestions Seriously 25

Employee Appraisals
Solicit 360-Degree Feedback 26

Employee Compensation
Grant Stock Options to All Employees 27
Limit Wage Disparity 29

Community Outreach
Help Publicize a Worthy Cause 30
Encourage Employee Volunteerism 31
Organize an Event to Benefit the Community 34
Join With Other Businesses to Support the Community 35

Work and Family
Make the Workplace Family-Friendly 36

Doing Business Abroad
Support Alternative Trade Organizations 39
Commit to International Business Principles 40

Civic Participation
Get Employees Out to Vote 41

Environmental Responsibility
Replant or Donate Living Christmas Trees 42
Use Recycled, Unbleached Paper 43
Use Shredded Documents as Packing Material 44
Send a Monthly E-mail With 'Green Tips' 45
Commit to Environmental Principles 47

Other Awareness Ideas
Suggest and Loan Books from the Company Library 49
Create Wallet Cards 49
Hold Creative Contests for Employees 50
Sponsor Art/Essay Contests for Employees' Kids 51
Display 'Table Tents' in the Lunchroom 52

Online Resources 53

Part 2: Effective Ethics Codes

Introduction: Ethics Codes Don't Make People Ethical
    by Michael Josephson 57

Ten Benefits of Having an Ethics Code 58

Making the Code Effective 59

Starting With a Values Statement 60

What an Ethics Code Should Say 61

Interpreting Behavioral Regulations 70

Language 71

Appendix: Sample Ethics Codes and Documents

A Letter to Employees from the Head of the Company 75

Corporate Values Statement ("Our Credo," Johnson & Johnson) 77

Environmental Values Statement ("Environmental Mission Statement,"
    Starbucks Coffee Company) 79

Guidelines for Doing Business Abroad ("Global Sourcing and Operating
    Guidelines," Levi Strauss & Company) 80

Whistleblower Protections ("Retaliation Against Informants,"
    Sarbanes-Oxley Act, 2002) 84

Guidelines for Whistleblowing ("Responsibility and Consequences,"
    Northrop Grumman's "Standards of Business Conduct") 85

Model Code for Business ("The Caux Round Table Principles
    for Business") 86

Compiled Ethics Codes: A Sampling of Topics 94

Resources on Ethics Codes 110

——— Introduction ———

There is no silver bullet for creating an ethical workplace. Anyone who seeks to create a culture of personal and social responsibility, of openness and integrity, does it best by personally setting an example — not by giving orders.

Still, it is important to communicate expectations, standards and a solid commitment to ethics. Companies can draft a code of conduct, for example, but Enron had one too — over 60 pages of provisions that obviously had little effect on decision-making in the executive suites. If senior managers don't walk the talk — especially when doing the right thing calls for a heavy sacrifice — then codes and credos are bound to spur cynicism and erode morale. Similarly, practices like those in this book can promote ethics in the workplace, but if employees sense a lack of candor and feel day-to-day disdain, even the best-conceived programs will flop.

The first part of this book presents these "good ideas," which companies around the country are using to fortify their character. Part two discusses how to draft and implement effective ethics codes, and the appendix presents examples of codes that companies are using today.

Nowadays, corporate ethics initiatives are more popular than ever. The Sarbanes-Oxley Act of 2002, and the wave of scandals that precipitated it, spurred this trend. The Act requires companies to tighten up internal controls and file statements with the SEC on their ethics codes for financial officers. It also mandated that the U.S. Sentencing Commission review its guidelines on what constitutes an "effective compliance and ethics program." In 2004, the Commission released revised guidelines that charged CEOs with promoting "an organizational culture that encourages ethical conduct."

Building this ethical culture is the key. Fulfilling legal requirements is important, but a mere compliance mentality can promote a false sense of security, putting you at even greater risk. That's because "wrongdoing" is an ethical concept even more than a legal one. Accusations alone can harm reputations, hamper the ability to attract top talent, and divert attention from running an efficient business.

Leadership training in ethics is also basic to sustaining a successful organization. The Josephson Institute offers the nation's premier seminars to help leaders transform workplace cultures. In addition to providing private business consulting services, the Institute conducts specialized programs for city/county managers, law enforcement and school administrators.

The nonprofit, nonpartisan Institute focuses on what works in the real world. Its unique approach also stresses the value of collaboration, with numerous services for a wide range of institutions — public, educational, nonprofit, human-service and corporate — reinforcing individual ethics initiatives. Other Institute projects include: CHARACTER COUNTS!, the nation's most widely implemented approach to character education, and the Pursuing Victory With Honor sportsmanship campaign, endorsed by major American amateur athletic groups. All projects offer training programs and support materials.

We encourage readers to share their own best practices for inclusion in future editions of this book. Send your correspondence via e-mail or regular mail, and visit the Institute online.

Josephson Institute of Ethics
Dept. of Publications and Communications
9841 Airport Blvd., Suite 300, Los Angeles, CA 90045
www.josephsoninstitute.org; www.charactercounts.org
(310) 846-4800 or (800) 711-2670

To help individuals improve, the Institute seeks to:
- Stimulate moral ambition.
- Heighten the ability to perceive the ethical dimension of choices.
- Teach how to discern the most effective ethical responses.
- Show how to implement these responses intelligently.

The Institute enhances organizational ethics by helping leaders to:
- Identify the ethical obligations arising from positions of authority.
- Consider the impact of all institutional actions on all stakeholders.
- Create workplaces that reward ethical and discourage unethical conduct.

The Institute's services include:
- Presentations and keynote addresses
- Workshops, seminars and community forums
- Customized on-site training
- Ethics audits and consulting, including services related to standards/codes of conduct
- Media commentary
- Ethics and Effectiveness in the Workplace seminars
- Character Development Seminars
- *Pursuing Victory With Honor* sportsmanship seminars
- *Honor Above All* academic integrity materials
- *Foundations for Life* quotation-based essay contest
- Publications, videos and communications

The Six Pillars of Character

The Six Pillars of Character — *trustworthiness, respect, responsibility, fairness, caring* and *citizenship* — are core ethical values that transcend race, religion, gender and politics. The Institute encourages organizations to use these values as ground rules for making decisions. Each idea in this book stresses at least one of these Pillars, as noted in the top corner of each page.

Trustworthiness
- Honesty in communications (truthfulness, sincerity and candor)
- Honesty in conduct (not stealing or cheating)
- Integrity
- Reliability (promise-keeping)
- Loyalty

Respect
- Civility, courtesy and decency
- Autonomy
- Tolerance

Responsibility
- Accountability
- Pursuit of excellence (diligence and perseverance)
- Self-restraint

Fairness
- Impartiality
- Equity

Caring
- Charity
- Compassion

Citizenship
- Volunteerism; doing your share
- Environmental protection
- Law abidance

PART ONE

Good Ideas for Creating an Ethical Workplace

IDEA #1
Keep Employees Informed

Be candid with employees about the company's prospects — where opportunities are growing and waning. If layoffs loom, or if the skills of some workers may become obsolete, they should learn about it as early as possible. Moreover, the company should do all it can to demonstrate compassion and commitment to its staff by offering counseling and retraining. When management seems less than forthright with its employees, cynicism and suspicion increase. Morale and company loyalty also suffer when management imposes "restructuring" schemes on the workforce without warning. *Here are a few examples of how companies are seeking to be open about these matters*:

> *If [employees] are kept out of the picture . . . rumors and fear proliferate. When the first wave of layoffs comes, the cuts will seem arbitrary and ruthless.*
>
> — Lesley Wright and Marti Smye, consultants and authors of *Corporate Abuse* (Macmillan, 1996)

• Intel offers courses to all members of the staff on the company's financial and competitive picture. For those whose jobs may be in jeopardy, the company offers training programs, teaching skills to help them succeed there or elsewhere.

• Sun Microsystems is one of many companies offering general career management courses. Sun even has opened a career center to test job skills and interests and discuss prospects with in-house counselors.

• Texas Instruments has a program to train employees whose skills may soon be obsolete. Chuck Nielson, vice president of human resources, says the company used to have employees "out on the sidewalk before they knew what hit them." Now, he says, "We tell them, 'This job won't be here in a year. What do we need to do to broaden [your skills] to look for a job inside or outside TI?'"

IDEA #2
Encourage Candid Employee Feedback

Open and honest communication needs to come from low-level employees as well as senior managers. It shouldn't depend on workplace gimmicks, but some incentives can help. *Examples*:

- Carillon Importers of Teaneck, New Jersey, and Air France teamed up to improve communication between employees and managers. The program, called "Team Talk," encourages workers to call a toll-free number to answer employee surveys and leave comments and suggestions for managers. In addition to earning travel points redeemable from Air France, some callers are "instant winners," capturing prizes such as telephones and radios.

- Home Depot, Inc. holds quarterly meetings transmitted via satellite from the headquarters to stores across the country. Employees are paid to attend and hear the company's leaders answer phoned-in questions from employees and discuss the past quarter's performance and new plans and ideas. Says one regional manager, "The best thing about these broadcasts is that workers see that [senior executives] aren't afraid to share company details. In most companies there are sensitive topics that high officers want to sidestep, but not here. It makes people feel like they know exactly what's going on."

> *You've got to keep your mouth shut. You can't tell them your opinion. You have to do everything they say. The Disney way. Never say anything negative. Everything's positive. There's never a no.*
>
> — A Disney Corp. employee, as reported in Jane Kuenz's *Inside the Mouse* (Duke University Press, 1995)

- Great Western Drilling Company in Midland, Texas, offers $25 to the employee who poses the most challenging question to the president at the company communication meetings.

IDEA #3
Clarify the Code of Conduct

When the Arizona Public Service Company initiated a comprehensive ethics program in the mid-1990's, its ethics officers provided senior managers instruction guides and videotaped training instructions along with copies of the company's lengthy code of conduct. Then they asked managers to call or send e-mail — and to have those under their supervision do the same — if there were questions about the code. Queries flooded in, and to manage them the company developed the "ComplianceGram." Herbert Zinn, principal architect of the program, outlines the system:

1. When the employee makes an inquiry about compliance (usually by phone or e-mail), he/she is contacted personally to ensure a complete understanding of the question. Often an answer is provided verbally and immediately followed up with a written confirmation. This serves as a reminder to employees in case some of the answer is forgotten and it enables them to consider the response at length.

2. Employees are instructed to pass on the information and post the written response in a conspicuous location for all to see.

3. Periodically, all inquiries are merged into one e-mail and transmitted to department managers. They review points that are relevant to their operations and discuss them with staff members.

Although the process is time-consuming, Mr. Zinn reports several advantages:

*   By committing considerable resources, the company demonstrates its seriousness about ethical compliance.

*   It gives the program high visibility.

*   It helps compliance officers gauge the effectiveness and extent of the program's implementation.

*   It provides a record of the company's good-faith efforts to administer a comprehensive ethics program.

IDEA #4
Offer Hotlines for Ethical Guidance or Whistleblowing

According to the Ethics Resource Center, many companies have established whistleblower hotlines, but 65 to 85 percent of these calls are from employees simply needing guidance or advice. Many companies, such as Motorola and Sears, report that it has been easier and more effective to set up a separate means (often e-mail) of responding to inquiries about the company's code of conduct or other matters of ethical concern. *Two other examples*:

- Jacquelyn Gates, vice president of NYNEX's ethics and business practices department, reports that half of the calls deal with human-resources issues (e.g., benefits, job evaluations); 40 percent are for guidance on gray areas (for example, potential conflicts of interest); and 3 to 7 percent involve direct allegations of wrongdoing (whistleblowing). The NYNEX number is available every day at all hours because their internal research shows that people tend not to report critical issues during the workday.

- Raytheon compliance officers say they receive approximately 100 calls a month. Eighty percent involve minor issues that can be resolved on the spot while the remainder are split evenly between those seeking advice and those reporting a serious ethical lapse that requires senior management attention.

IDEA #5

Issue Corporate Accountability Reports

American University professor Ralph Estes, in his *Tyranny of the Bottom Line* (Berrett Koehler, 1996), argues that all firms should voluntarily make available "corporate accountability reports" (through the mail, on the Internet and in company reception areas). At a minimum, he proposes that companies should be candid with the public about:

Customer Information Needs

1. *Records of legal and regulatory claims* brought against the corporation (e.g., how the company has settled customer complaints about products, a record of citations and indictments for regulatory violations)

2. *Product information* (e.g., the safety of packaging and contents for the environment)

3. *Social responsibility information* (e.g., labor and human rights considerations in country where product was produced)

Worker Information Needs

1. *Employment security and stability* (e.g., plans for restructuring and for easing the pains of downsizing for affected employees)

2. *Health and safety* (e.g., job risks, medical statistics related to workplace injuries)

3. *Employment data* (e.g., employee turnover, opportunities for advancement)

4. *Employee grievances*

5. *Impact of technology*

6. *Worker satisfaction with pension programs and other benefits*

Community Information Needs

1. *Ownership of the corporation* (e.g., who owns large blocks of stock)

2. *Financial data* (i.e., information disclosed on SEC Form 10-K)

3. *Relevant corporate history* (e.g., legal cases, arrangements with city planners)

4. *Impact on community infrastructure* (e.g., how the company's expansion or relocation will affect schools, automobile traffic, waste collection)

5. *Taxes paid at all levels*

6. *Materials used, transported and stored*

7. *Job creation data*

8. *Investments*

9. *Contributions* (charitable and political, including lobbying efforts)

IDEA #6
Conduct Social and Environmental Responsibility Audits

The New Economics Foundation (NEF), a London-based nonprofit organization, assesses how well an organization adheres to key principles of social justice and environmental sustainability. NEF helps design, guide and monitor a company's self-evaluation in these areas and prepares an auditor's report to critique it and make recommendations.

Ben & Jerry's has been publishing what it now calls "social and environmental assessments" since 1988 and has commissioned the services of NEF and SustainAbility, an international firm that specializes in environmental consulting. The ice cream maker says these elements are essential to the social/environmental audit process (see recent reports at www.benandjerrys.com):

- *Dialogue with stakeholders* (staff, customers, beneficiaries of company's community outreach programs, shareholders, suppliers, franchisees). Use focus groups and periodic surveys for this purpose.

- *Performance indicators.* These are specific measurements of performance relative to each stakeholder group. Refine and augment these over time.

- *External benchmarks.* Where possible, compare internal performance measurements against external benchmarks. The sources of external benchmarks vary and are limited by what is available and useful.

- *Management comments and commitments.* The CEO and other senior officers should address key issues in the audit, providing comments and announcing specific goals for the coming year.

- *External audit.* An outside firm should review the company's audit at least every few years and make recommendations to achieve objectives and improve the process. The NEF convenes an Audit

Advisory Group, comprised of independent people with expertise in relevant areas. In addition to making recommendations, this group checks the accuracy and completeness of the company's internal audit.

The New Economics Foundation (NEF)
Vine Court, 112-116 Whitechapel Rd., London, E1 1JE, UK
www.neweconomics.org
phone: 011-44-171-377-5696

SustainAbility
20-22 Bedford Row, London, WC1R 4EBUK
(with offices in Washington, D.C. and San Francisco)
www.sustainability.co.uk

IDEA #7
Use Core Ethical Values as Audit Criteria

Example:

The national office of the YMCA in Chicago had its accounting firm rate the organization's transactions to the degree that they were *honest*, *responsible*, *caring* and *fair*. All staff members and volunteers completed surveys on how well the organization puts these stated values into practice. (In addition, all full-time staff members spent a day-and-a-half with an independent consultant to gauge the organization's ethical health.) The YMCA shared aggregate results of the surveys with employees and asked them for suggestions on how the organization could improve. "We want to hold ourselves accountable," says Ron Kinnamon, then the assistant executive national director of the 13-million member group. "The very process sent a message. Everyone involved with us became more aware of our commitment to 'walk our talk' — even the accounting firm. We're going to change their culture too!"

> *The very process sent a message. Everyone involved with us became more aware of our commitment to 'walk our talk.'*
>
> — Ron Kinnamon,
> assistant executive
> national director, YMCA USA

IDEA #8
Manage With an Open Book

All employees should be accountable to one another for their performances. Opening the company books to the staff is one way to increase accountability and efficiency, in addition to reducing employee suspicions. Making everyone's salary public knowledge is probably taking it too far, but some companies have benefitted by encouraging employees to monitor expenditures. *Examples*:

*   At ReManufacturing Corporation in Springfield, Michigan, employees can scrutinize all aspects of corporate finance and operations. The company even pays for employees to attend classes so they can learn how to interpret the figures. As employees track their collective progress, they receive incentives (bonuses and stock) to contribute ideas that enhance the company's competitive position. ReManufacturing CEO Jack Stack, has achieved much success with this open-book system and consults with and speaks to other managers about implementing it in their organizations.

    > *An approach to running a company that gets everyone thinking like an owner instead of a hired hand.*
    >
    > — "Open-Book Management," as defined by John Case in his book of the same name (Harper Business, 1995)

*   Atkinson-Baker & Associates, a Los Angeles court reporting firm, has each of its 50 employees track a key financial statistic relating to his or her job each day. The company processes these figures daily and each week produces a graph showing over two dozen financial trends. As CEO Alan Atkinson-Baker told *Business Ethics* magazine, "I think employees like it because it's predictable for them. If they put in for a pay raise, they can see for themselves how they are producing. It doesn't become a personality issue."

IDEA #9

Issue Guidelines to Recruiters and Interviewers

Employees sense how committed an organization is to ethics even before their first day on the job. During interviews and in the recruiting process, prospective employees should be told in no uncertain terms that ethical conduct is the first responsibility of all the company's members. (Then, of course, senior management must do all it can to *demonstrate* their commitment.) Consider sharing these ethical guidelines with recruiters and interviewers:

The Employer Must:

1. Hire in a way that does not promote discrimination of any kind.

2. Accurately represent the organization.

3. Offer a salary that is within an accepted, appropriate range for the position.

4. Honor employment offers.

5. Allow candidates ample time to make a decision. Be respectful of their desire to interview with other companies.

6. In summary, be truthful!

The Candidate Must:

1. Have a sincere interest in pursuing a position with that firm (don't accept a company's offer and keep interviewing; don't renege on an acceptance; don't play firms against one another).

2. Be honest and open about future plans (e.g., graduate or law school, transfer/relocation requests).

3. Honor any guidelines that have been established between the school

and employer.

4. Be honest and open about salary or decision date information.

5. Make a legitimate effort to respond within the agreed-upon time frame.

6. In summary, be truthful!

IDEA #10

Show Respect and Sensitivity in Terminations

Unfortunately, firms occasionally have to terminate employees. When doing so, use the following pointers:

- Document incidents as they occur and get the facts. Don't let rumors and secondhand information cloud performance assessments.

- Ensure direct and timely communication with the employee; no one should be fired without knowing why.

- Be sure to warn employees whose performance needs improvement. Then give them a reasonable amount of time to reverse course.

- Timing is critical. Try to ensure that the worker has some private time immediately after you give him the news.

- Keep plans quiet. Co-workers shouldn't be giving tips and spreading rumors about another's fate.

- Do not try to make light of the situation with jokes or other attempts at amusement.

- Do it face-to-face, not with an impersonal pink slip.

- Do it privately. Humiliating someone in front of co-workers is inexcusable.

- No matter how incompetent, unreliable or poorly mannered the terminated person has been, do your best to empathize and show sensitivity — not because she or he is a respectable person, but because *you* are.

IDEA #11
Manage Diversity Effectively

According to a 2003 *New York Times* survey, companies that call themselves "diversity friendly" have an advantage in the recruiting marketplace. Job seekers and recruiters in the survey overwhelmingly agreed that diversity initiatives, no matter how diversity is defined, are "extremely important." Among job seekers, 91 percent said that diversity programs make an organization a better place to work.

These days most large companies have some kind of diversity initative. But not all of the programs are equal. Here are some guidelines that diversity management consultants recommend:

> *The wrong question: How are we doing on race relations? The right question: Is this a workplace where 'we' is everyone?*
>
> — R. Roosevelt Thomas, Jr., director of the American Institute for Managing Diversity, Inc.

- Clearly communicate to the staff the importance of respecting cultural differences, and how it improves the workplace. For instance, it creates more effective communication among staff, with customers, and between workers and management; greater productivity; and less turnover in a more comfortable working environment).

- Assess the company's culture, perhaps by surveying the staff, and determine what changes you need to make. Examine whether or not the company's personnel policies really encourage respect for diversity.

- Ensure that top management is visibly involved and at the forefront in combatting divisiveness.

- Make expectations clear and let everyone know they will be held accountable (and follow through!).

- Develop criteria to measure progress.

- R. Roosevelt Thomas, Jr., director of the American Institute for Managing Diversity, recommends applying this test to all company policies: Does it give special consideration to one group? Will it contribute to everyone's success, or will it only produce an advantage for a single racial or gender group? Could anyone perceive it as something for *them* as opposed to *us*? Says Mr. Thomas: "Whenever the answer is yes, you're not yet on the road to managing diversity."

The American Institute for Managing Diversity in Atlanta conducts "cultural audits" and makes recommendations to companies on how to increase respect for diversity in the workplace. Visit www.aimd.org or call 404-756-1170.

IDEA #12
Guarantee Fair Treatment

Example:

- The Marriott Corporation developed a program (now emulated by Federal Express) that encourages employees to file grievances if they witness unfair treatment or feel like they are victims of it. Known as Guaranteed Fair Treatment (GFT), the program's review board often grants bonuses to those who report unfair practices in the workplace.

IDEA #13

Promote Tolerance

While few people openly admit to being racists or misogynists, studies show that many remain unabashedly hostile toward homosexuals. As part of their diversity-management programs, some companies have developed workshops that focus specifically on this form of intolerance. *Examples*:

• At AT&T's largest factory in the Catholic and blue-collar bastion of North Andover, Massachusetts, some 2,000 employees have voluntarily attended a workshop called "Homophobia in the Workplace." Among the numerous diversity trainings offered, the workshop consistently ranks No. 1 in employee surveys. Brian McNaught, an openly gay author and professional trainer who conducts the workshop, says he makes no effort to win over anyone on moral or religious grounds; his objective is simply to make the workplace a "welcome environment" for all. As personnel manager Sheila Landers told *The Wall Street Journal*, the training stays with many after they leave the plant. "I've had colleagues tell me it's made a difference in their lives," she says.

• A growing number of companies are backing up anti-homophobia workshops by offering domestic partner benefits to same-sex couples. AOL-Time Warner, Microsoft, IBM and Sprint are among the many large corporations that extend benefits to gay and lesbian partners and their children.

IDEA #14
Give Awards for Employee Excellence

There's nothing novel about giving "employee excellence" awards, but firms often see "excellence" in narrow, bottom-line terms. If your organization has a values statement — and the vast majority of big companies do — why not use those values as the criteria for a prestigious annual Employee Excellence Award? *Example*:

- The Washington, D.C.-based Marriott Corporation honors over a dozen people a year with its J. Willard Marriott Award of Excellence. Winners receive a medallion engraved with the company values: dedication, achievement, character, ideals, effort and perseverance. Honorees — from dishwashers to housekeepers to merchandise managers — are nominated by co-workers and recognized at an annual banquet in Washington.

IDEA #15
Tell the Company's Story

Example:

• At Armstrong International in Stuart, Florida, the company's walls tell stories. The firm frames parables written by employees and displays them in the hallways. Every six months it collects new stories in a booklet and distributes it to all staff members. Company COO David Armstrong, who conceived of the idea, told *Business Ethics* that "the stories chosen must reflect the teller's style of management and the company's 'morals.'" He noted a few other guidelines and tips:

  • Start with positive stories and always name the individual.

  • Keep the story to one page.

  • Use simple but active language.

  • Do not use the individual's name in negative stories.

  • Retell stories — they keep the past culture alive and related to the present.

IDEA #16
Take Employee Suggestions Seriously

The suggestion box is a fixture in many offices. But according to a recent survey only 41 percent of employees believe the average company listens to workers' ideas. While many businesses reward people who contribute outstanding ideas, the criteria for such perks tend to focus on boosting productivity and profits — not principles. Bob Nelson, in his *1001 Ways to Reward Employees*, lists dozens of innovative programs, a couple of which encourage employees to help create a more ethical work environment. *Example*:

- The General Mills "Championship Way" program at the company's Minneapolis headquarters has employees from different departments gather periodically to discuss how to increase accountability and reduce blameshifting. The General Mills values statement serves as a guide and filter for suggestions. Small groups meet later to discuss how to implement the ideas. Finally, the company rewards employees who make the most helpful suggestions.

What about employees who make suggestions but believe management has passed them over for rewards? *Here's an idea for making the process fair*:

- Eastman Kodak in Rochester, New York, tries to encourage employees to contribute money-saving ideas by rewarding them with 15 percent of the savings achieved in the first two years of the idea's implementation. If an employee's idea results in a new product, he or she receives 3 percent of its sales in the first year. Kodak reportedly has given awards — averaging $3 million annually — to more than 30,000 people.

IDEA #17
Solicit 360-Degree Feedback

Include subordinates as well as bosses in performance reviews. Proponents of this "360-degree feedback" don't usually recommend hinging pay raises and promotions on these reviews, but they say this process helps identify training needs and foster an atmosphere of openness and fairness. Multiple anonymous appraisers may enhance the credibility of the review. Before implementing this system, most companies say they coach all staff members on being impartial and honest in reviews. Companies using this strategy include Baxter International, AT&T and Dow Chemical.

> *Some of our supervisors are by nature very responsive to people above them, but less responsive to people at the same level or below. I've noticed a change now, as they realize they're going to be evaluated by these people.*
>
> — Gary Dyer, president of Farm Credit, a lending cooperative where 360-degree reviews constitute about half the annual performance-review process (quoted in *The Wall Street Journal*)

IDEA #18
Grant Stock Options to All Employees

Former Labor Secretary Robert Reich advocates granting stock options to all employees as a way to "allow workers to share the gain as well as the pain." Everyone at the company shares both risks and rewards.

PepsiCo, Starbucks, Southwest Airlines and Cisco are among the growing number of large, publicly-traded companies that give stock options to most or all of their employees. In 2001, the National Center for Employee Ownership (NCEO) estimated that up to 10 million employees received stock options.

> *Sixty percent of companies report improved productivity after instituting employee stock ownership programs.*
>
> — Employee Stock Ownership Plan Association

Examples:

- PepsiCo grants all its employees stock options equal to 10 percent of their previous year's pay. They can exercise options over the following five to 10 years. This policy started in 1989.

- San Jose-based Cisco Systems Inc., which allows all of its employees to participate in a stock ownership plan, attributes much of its success — including one of the lowest turnover rates in the industry and extremely high revenue per employee — to participatory management and its stock ownership plan. As Mary Thurber, Cisco's manager of investor relations, told *Business Ethics*, "Diligent employees who work as a team have the mission of Cisco as their goal. That makes us interact a lot better with the customer, and that's good for business."

- BankAmerica's employee stock option program is open to most hourly and part-time employees as well as the corporation's salaried workers. Even a bank teller who works five hours a week is eligible to purchase from 50 to 90 shares every six months for three years.

- Procter & Gamble, Whole Foods, Walgreens, Wendy's and several pharmaceutical companies also have made stock options an integral part of compensation packages for workers at various levels.

The National Center for Employee Ownership (NCEO)
(510) 208-1300; nceo@nceo.org; www.nceo.org

IDEA #19
Limit Wage Disparity

While the average worker takes home $517 a week, CEOs of top American corporations earn over $150,000 weekly, says a 2003 report in *BusinessWeek*. And according to compensation consulting firm Pearl Meyer & Partners, in 2004 the average CEO's compensation was $9.97 million.

These figures have fueled shareholder and board initiatives to limit executive compensation. Companies that have imposed salary ceilings often cite issues of fairness and employee morale, in addition to concerns about company expenditures.

Example:

- At Bagel Works, Inc., management recognizes that huge income disparities are not only unfair, but demoralizing. Bagel Works limits the highest salary to 3.5 times what the *lowest* paid worker receives.

IDEA #20

Help Publicize a Worthy Cause

According to a study by Cone Communications and Roper Starch Worldwide, nearly one-third of consumers say they consider a company's social responsibility when making purchasing decisions. Over half said they would pay more for a product if it supported a cause they cared about and about two-thirds said they would switch brands or retailers to support a cause they cared about. Not surprisingly, many companies have found that marketing their products and services alongside a worthy cause (while giving it more than just verbal support) is a hit for all parties involved. *Example*:

• In 1993 Avon Products founded the Avon Worldwide Fund for Women's Health, a global initiative whose biggest program is the Breast Cancer Awareness Crusade in the United States. Through the Awareness Crusade, the company's half-million-member sales force educates women by bringing brochures, pens and pins along on sales visits. Sales of merchandise such as the pins and pens have raised over $16 million for community-based breast cancer education and early detection services. The company is confident that the program has boosted sales, but as Joanne Mazurki, director of the Awareness Crusade, told *Business Ethics*, "We view this program as a brand building technique, not a sales generating technique."

IDEA #21
Encourage Employee Volunteerism

A company can plainly show it cares about doing *good* as much as doing *well* by committing resources and time to support the community. Ideally, this means sending not just money, but employees — on company time. *Examples*:

- For decades, Coldwell Banker has participated in Habitat for Humanity's universally praised mission — to build simple, decent and affordable homes in partnership with deserving families. Employees from hundreds of Coldwell Banker offices across the country support the work of this nonprofit group in a variety of ways: from promotion (e.g., distributing stickers, pins, notepads, postcards and brochures) to fundraising (e.g., tournaments, raffles, collection jars and collective employee garage sales) to supporting Habitat volunteers (e.g., sponsoring parties) to actually hammering nails to construct quality housing for low-income families.

- Perot Systems offered to donate $120,000 in groceries and toys to inner-city residents — if employees delivered them personally. The company wanted workers to "walk the talk" by contributing time and energy rather than just money. In addition, the personnel department created a new division to help employees arrange afternoons off to teach English-as-a-second-language classes or to volunteer at senior or day-care centers.

- Ben & Jerry's Community Action Teams (CATs) consist of employees who are elected by their co-workers to make small grants to local community organizations and to organize service projects that involve local Ben & Jerry's employees. To get staff members involved in corporate philanthropy, the company maintains a nine-member Employee Foundation Committee to make grantmaking decisions. Chosen by their co-workers and representing various sectors of the company, the members of this committee serve three-year terms, staggered to ensure continuity.

- McCormick & Company, Inc., a manufacturer of seasonings and frozen foods, holds its annual "Charity Day" on a Saturday and encourages employees to show up at work and donate their pay (provided at time-and-a-half by the company) to a favorite charity. More than 90 percent of the staff participates. The company also matches its employees' charitable contributions dollar for dollar.

- After seven years of service, Intel employees may apply for half a year off, with pay, to pursue public service or teaching.

- If a Levi Strauss employee actively participates for a year in a community organization, the company's foundation will donate $500 to that group. A nonprofit organization with a Levi Strauss employee on its board will receive a grant of $500, $1,000 or $1,500 depending on the size of its budget.

- The Los Angeles-based Atlantic Richfield Company (ARCO) holds an annual community service awards ceremony for its employees.

- Through the AT&T CARES (Community Awards Recognizing Employee Service) Grant Program, employees can apply for contributions to benefit the organizations where they volunteer. An employee may request up to three AT&T CARES individual grants of $250 each in a calendar year to three different organizations.

- In 1989, the Timberland Company started a relationship with City Year, a Boston-based "urban Peace Corps" that brings together young people from diverse backgrounds for a year of full-time community service. Timberland has since invested millions of dollars in City Year. Separately, through its Path of Service program, Timberland employees receive 40 hours of paid time off to serve in their communities.

- Clothes the Deal, a Los Angeles-based nonprofit, provides professional attire to homeless and other needy job seekers. The organization screens clients and offers them high-quality secondhand officewear to help them get jobs. To gather donations for Clothes the Deal, several local businesses hold clothing drives. Apparel stores have offered discounts on merchandise to customers who donate business suits, blouses and shirts. Nissan Motor Corp. USA and Honda Motors have also sponsored successful clothing drives for

Clothes The Deal. *For more information or to arrange a companywide clothing drive, visit www.clothesthedeal.org or contact Clothes the Deal at (818) 798-9186.*

• Kelsey's Pizzeria Eatery isn't in business just to make dough. The Orlando-based food chain has teamed up with a local middle school to combat youth violence by rewarding students with free pizza if they participate in discussions about guns and violence at school. The youngsters (and their parents) also must sign an anti-guns-at-school contract. *Kelsey's has also helped other businesses conduct similar programs. Contact them at (407) 671-1760.*

IDEA #22
Organize an Event to Benefit the Community

Examples:

- The Scooper Bowl — an annual summer ice cream festival with contributions by Baskin Robbins, Ben & Jerry's, Häagen-Dazs and many other ice cream makers — raised $157,000 in 2004 for the Jimmy Fund to help fight cancer at the Dana-Farber Cancer Institute and around the world. Since it began in 1983, the Scooper Bowl has served more than 200 tons of ice cream and raised more than $1.5 million for the Jimmy Fund.

- Coldwell Banker Action Realty in Cambridge, Minnesota, sponsored a marathon 100-hole golf tournament, which raised over $30,000 for Habitat for Humanity.

- Sun Microsystems designates an annual "worldwide volunteer week" for employees. The company says its employees clocked 6,800 volunteer hours in 2003. Since its inception in 1995 the program has engaged over 10,000 Sun employees in service projects that supported over 1,000 schools and nonprofits worldwide.

- Intel Foundation works with schools in various communities to offer awards for "Innovations in Teaching" and "Excellence in Teaching."

- Sprint's "Inner Circle" mentoring program pairs black professionals at the company with African-American students in nearby communities.

- Fleet Financial, a Boston-based investment company, sponsors a "mini-MBA" program to teach entrepreneurial skills to inner-city youth, who learn the basics of supply and demand, bookkeeping and cost/benefit analysis.

IDEA #23
Join With Other Businesses to Support the Community

Example:

• When the District of Columbia's city government terminated its recycling program, members of Business for Social Responsibility stepped in to replace it. Also, companies affiliated with this organization and with the Co-op America Business Network joined forces to sponsor a clean-up day for the Chesapeake and Ohio Canal.

Business for Social Responsibility
1683 Folsom Street
San Francisco, CA 94103-3722
(415) 865-2500; bsr@bsr.org; www.bsr.org

Co-op America Business Network
1612 K St., NW, #600
Washington, DC 20006
(202) 872-5307; www.coopamerica.org

IDEA #24
Make the Workplace Family-Friendly

When AT&T surveyed its senior managers about their chief anxieties, "it turned out that teenagers were the number-one concern off the job and the number-one distraction on the job," a company spokesperson told *The Wall Street Journal*. But child care, elder care and even personal physical fitness are also concerns. To keep employees happy and healthy — which, according to Working Mother Media CEO Carol Evans, translates into boosted productivity, less absenteeism and fewer health care and disability expenses for the company — more and more companies are trying to ease the special burdens of working parents.

> **Fifty-four percent.**
>
> — Childless employees willing to contribute part of their income to on-site child care. (1996 Gallup poll of 702 employed Americans)

Examples of family-friendly ideas:

* At its Minneapolis headquarters, General Mills provides extensive services for working mothers. In addition to maternity leave and flexible hours, the company offers on-site child care and health facilities with nutritionists and personal trainers.

* Motorola contracts with BabyLink, a telephone resource and referral service with obstetrical nurses available 24 hours to answer questions. Before the arrangement, 48 Motorola employees experienced prenatal complications. After two years of the service, this number shrunk to 23. The result: less stressful pregnancies and significant savings for the company.

> **Twenty-five to 30 percent.**
>
> — For the working parent making $30,000 or less, the average portion of household income spent on child care.

- After paying $1.1 million in medical bills to cover five premature births, Sunbeam Oster Household Products began to pay pregnant workers at the company's Louisiana plant to attend maternity classes twice a month. The self-insured plant's average medical costs per birth dropped from $27,000 in 1984 to $3,500 in 1990, and there were no premature births among the 450 female employees in that period.

- Opening an on-site child-care facility isn't just for corporate giants. For example, VCW Inc., a Kansas City insurance company, opened one in 1989 when it had little more than two dozen employees — and only four children to occupy the center. (Today, with 75 VCW employees, the number of kids there has increased threefold.) Consultants who service small businesses (as well as large ones) interested in exploring this option are mushrooming. A few that are mentioned in a recent *Wall Street Journal* article: Corporate Family Solutions in Nashville; Dependent Care Connection in Westport, Connecticut; Bright Horizons Children's Centers in Cambridge, Massachusetts; and Partnership Group in Blue Bell, Pennsylvania.

> **Many children, even very young ones, are 'punching in' for a full-time child-care week.**
>
> — Jeff Capizzano of the Urban Institute, a Washington, D.C., nonprofit organization. The Institute reported in a 2005 study that half of children under five years old with mothers working full-time spend at least 35 hours a week in child care.

- Rejuvenation, an Oregon-based company, donates $100 to each public school attended by its employees' children ($100 per employee, with the contributions earmarked for classroom activities).

- In the past two years, AT&T has spent more than $2 million to support community after-school programs, including two pilot projects that enlist teenagers as volunteers in water conservation and elder-care programs.

- Parents making less than $30,000 a year typically spend 25 to 30 percent of their household income on child care. Tom's of Maine, a manufacturer of personal-care products, tries to meet this challenge by giving its lower paid workers child-care subsidies. The $9,000-

a-year program, according to a company spokesperson, enables moms and dads to pick higher-quality child care.

- Companies unable to provide specific child-care referrals may wish to share with their staff the number of a nonprofit, nationwide "resource and referral" service called Child Care Aware (www.childcareaware.org; 800-424-2246). The group provides working parents with a list of licensed child-care providers in their area.

Families and Work Institute
267 Fifth Ave., Floor 2
New York, NY 10016
(212) 465-2044
www.familiesandwork.org

Working Mother Media, Inc.
(publisher of *Working Mother* magazine)
www.workingmother.com

See the "Work & Family" column at CareerJournal.com, *The Wall Street Journal*'s "Executive Career Site":
www.careerjournal.com/columnists/workfamily

IDEA #25
Support Alternative Trade Organizations

Seeking to counter unfair and exploitative practices linked to international trade, Alternative Trade Organizations (ATOs) focus on developing the economies of the world's poorest communities, paying higher-than-average prices to artisans and farmers and selling their products through catalogs and in stores. Other ways ATOs benefit workers in the developing world:

- teaching the safe and sustainable use of environmental resources

- reaching out to groups typically excluded from export markets (e.g., rural cooperatives, women, disabled people and refugees)

- encouraging developments in housing, healthcare and education

ATOs often work in partnership with multinational companies operating in these developing regions. To find out how your company can support various ATO activities, contact:

The Fair Trade Federation
1612 K St., NW, Suite 600
Washington, DC 20006
(202) 872-5338
www.fairtradefederation.org

The Fair Trade Foundation
65 Landing Rd.
Higganum, CT 06441
(203) 345-3374

International Fair Trade Association
Prijssestraat 24
4101 CR Culemborg
The Netherlands
www.ifat.org

IDEA #26
Commit to International Business Principles

Examples:

- ## The Caux Round Table Principles for Business

  This document sets forth "a world standard against which business behavior can be measured," and the Caux Round Table encourages companies to use it to write their own codes of ethical conduct. Initiated by a group of global corporate leaders who convened in Caux-sur-Montreux, Switzerland, in 1986, the Principles for Business were drafted at a 1994 meeting hosted by the Minnesota Center for Corporate Responsibility in Minneapolis. Since then, the document has been translated into seven languages and introduced around the world. *See the appendix for the complete text. For more information, visit: www.cauxroundtable.org.*

- ## Principles for Global Corporate Responsibility

  The New York-based Interfaith Center on Corporate Responsibility (ICCR) released this 28-page set of principles in 1995 to provide a standard for social responsibility in the international marketplace. *To read the Principles visit www.iccr.org or call ICCR at (212) 870-2295.*

- ## Verite

  "Verite" (short for "Verification in Trade and Export"), a Massachusetts-based nonprofit, monitors offshore labor conditions for U.S. companies that demand high standards from suppliers and vendors. *Visit www.verite.org or call (413) 253-9227.*

IDEA #27
Get Employees Out to Vote

Corporations can do a lot to get their employees out to vote and strengthen democracy. They have to be careful to be nonpartisan, since federal law forbids firms from endorsing candidates to their employees. But they can offer numerous incentives to spur employees to the polls and reward them for volunteering.

Examples:

> *What do I owe to my times, to my country, to my neighbors, to my friends? Such are the questions which a virtuous man ought often to ask himself.*
>
> — Johann Kaspar Lavater

- At Atlantic Golf in Annapolis, Maryland, the company has a get-out-the-vote effort among its 200 employees, and provides each of them with the candidates' voting records. The company also gives employees paid time off if they volunteer on Election Day, and enters every employee-voter's name into a drawing for a paid vacation day.

- Learning Matters in New York City gives each of its 15 employees who votes a paid vacation day to take whenever he or she wants. "I feel very strongly democracy is not instinctual. It's a learned behavior," says president John Merrow. "We put the country at risk when we don't vote."

- Northern Telecom's office in Nashville gives workers a few hours off on election day to cast ballots.

- Pancoast Temporary Services in Pittsburgh reports that several of their clients allow the temps to leave early so they can make it to the polls.

IDEA #28
Replant or Donate Living Christmas Trees

BetterWorld.com reports that more businesses are buying living Christmas trees for the holidays and replanting them in the new year. Consider making this an annual company tradition.

Announce the new policy to the staff and explain why you are spending a little more time and money to do this. You may want to include some of the "Facts About Trees" in a memo or on a flier in the lunchroom.

After the holidays, recruit the whole staff to spruce up the company grounds. If you have no place to put your tree, contact local schools or conservation clubs, Trees for Life (www.treesforlife.org; 316-945-6929) or TreePeople (www.treepeople.org; 818-753-4600).

Or consider renting a live tree from the Original Living Christmas Tree Company (503-813-TREE; www.livingchristmastrees.org).

Facts About Trees

- Some 25-30 million real Christmas trees are sold in the United States every year.
- About 500,000 acres are used to grow Christmas trees in the U.S. Each acre provides enough daily oxygen for 18 people.
- Approximately 330,000 real Christmas trees are sold via e-commerce or catalog and shipped to the customer.
- Real Christmas trees are grown in all 50 states and Canada. Eighty percent of artificial trees are manufactured in China.
- Humans are destroying an acre of forest every second.
- Throughout the world, we cut down trees 10 times faster than we replant them. In Africa, 29 trees are cut for every one replanted.
- In the early years of the United States, more than one-third of the land was forested. Now, nearly half of it is gone.
- The average tree produces 240 pounds of oxygen annually.
- From birth to death, the average tree absorbs as much carbon dioxide as is released from the burning of one ton of coal.

(Sources: National Christmas Tree Association, www.christree.org; Trees for Life, www.treesforlife.org)

IDEA #29
Use Recycled, Unbleached Paper

Recycling bins are commonplace at work, and many companies have effective recycling programs. But the process should start long before employees are throwing away bottles, cans and paper. *Buying* recycled products and reducing your use of disposable items is key.

There is now a greater variety of recycled-content paper products and the prices have come down. Simply search the Web for "recycled paper products" and you will find hundreds of vendors.

Also, purchase paper that is not bleached with chlorine. (When it decomposes, chlorine-bleached paper releases carcinogenic and other toxic agents.) Papers bleached without chlorine are just as high in quality as regular paper — and sometimes higher. Soy-based ink is also a good, nontoxic alternative.

Of course, these habits are important for their own sake, but they are also excellent ways to publicize a company's environmental commitment to customers and partners.

IDEA #30
Use Shredded Documents as Packing Material

One-third of all the garbage sent to landfills is packaging waste. *Business Ethics* reports that Real Goods Trading Company of Ukiah, California, uses the county government's shredded documents, otherwise bound for the landfill, as packing material for its alternative energy products. The approach is economical as well as ecologically responsible: warehouse manager David Fissel puts the savings at between $6,000 and $10,000 annually. Real Goods, which ships $7 million in merchandise each year, encloses a letter in each parcel explaining why it uses shredded documents rather than non-biodegradable, ozone-depleting styrofoam "peanuts."

The Yahoo! small-business directory includes a section on "Eco-Friendly Packaging," which lists many vendors. (Simply search for these keywords at Yahoo.com.)

IDEA #31
Send a Monthly E-mail With 'Green Tips'

Send a company-wide e-mail message once a month or so with tips on being environmentally responsible. For all the ideas you'll ever need (and more), see: *50 Simple Things You Can Do to Save the Earth,* the *Green Lifestyle Handbook, 1001 Ways You Can Heal the Earth,* and Co-op America's *National Green Pages.*

Of course, you should first set a good example with green practices in your own workplace. You might use the e-mail newsletter to announce new initiatives at work, such as:

* Substituting fluorescent lights for traditional bulbs or using bulbs with lower wattage, to save energy.

* Using ceramic coffee mugs instead of disposable cups.

* Offering commuter benefits to employees, including subsidized transit or vanpool passes, telework programs or shuttles. The EPA and Department of Transportation recognize the top companies that offer these benefits (see www.bestworkplacesforcommuters.gov for a "toolkit for employers").

For details and more suggestions on running an environment-friendly office, see www.greenchoices.org/office.html.

Here are a few green tips you can include in employee newsletters:

At home:

* Weatherstrip doors and windows.

* Install a low-flow shower head and don't take long showers.

* Place a brick in your toilet reservoir to take up space and save water each time you flush.

- Reduce the junk mail you receive. Remove your name from mailing lists by visiting www.dmaconsumers.org/consumerassistance.html or contacting:

  > Mail Preference Service
  > Direct Marketing Association
  > PO Box 643
  > Carmel, NY 10512

- Rather than wasting paper and plastic, use your own cloth or string shopping bag for groceries.

On the road:

- Drive less frequently. Avoid driving short distances that you could walk, or multiply chores done on any given trip.
- Properly inflate your car's tires. Under-inflated tires wear out faster and reduce fuel efficiency.
- Recycle used motor oil, anti-freeze and other automotive fluids.
- Cut back on using your car's air conditioner, a source of ozone-depleting CFCs.

IDEA #32

Commit to Environmental Principles

Examples:

- **CERES**

  The Coalition for Environmentally Responsible Economies (CERES) works in partnership with companies and nonprofits on a range of environmental issues. It has developed an environmental conduct code to serve as a baseline standard in the business world.

  Review its 10 principles and consider making a pledge to uphold them. Once you have, inform all employees of the company's commitment. A firm that endorses the CERES principles agrees to provisions in these areas: protection of the biosphere, sustainable use of natural resources, waste reduction, energy conservation, risk reduction, safe products and services, environmental restoration and informing the public. Over a dozen Fortune 500 firms — including Sunoco, General Motors, Polaroid, Arizona Public Service and H.B. Fuller — have signed on.

  > *Environmental concerns are like a great river, a river that's getting bigger and stronger all the time. All Fuller is doing is getting out of the backwater and into the fast central flow of the river. A lot of companies don't see the river yet. When they do, we'll be way ahead.*
  >
  > — Anthony Andersen, CEO, H.B. Fuller
  > (as quoted in Joel Makower's *Beyond the Bottom Line*, Simon & Schuster, 1994)

  In 1997, Ceres launched the Global Reporting Initiative (GRI), an international standard for corporate reporting on the "triple bottom line" of economic, social and environmental performance. GRI is now an independent international institution with over 640 participating companies worldwide.

CERES
99 Chauncy Street, 6th Floor
Boston, MA 02111
(617) 247-0700; www.ceres.org

• The Business Charter for Sustainable Development

Created by the International Chamber of Commerce (ICC), this set of 16 principles seeks to help businesses around the world improve their environmental records. The Paris-based ICC is a non-governmental organization with members in more than 130 countries.

For more information and the full text of the Charter:
www.bsdglobal.com/tools/principles_icc.asp

The International Chamber of Commerce (ICC):
www.iccwbo.org

IDEA #33
Suggest and Loan Books From the Company Library

Literature and film are excellent tools to stimulate ethical thinking in the business world. Companies might consider stocking a library with books — both fiction and nonfiction — that have something meaningful to say about the importance of good character and making ethical decisions. An office-wide e-mail or memo might periodically recommend to employees new additions as they come in.

IDEA #34
Create Wallet Cards

When companies distribute their codes of conduct and values statements to employees, what do the workers actually do with them? Some firms have found creative ways to reduce the chance of these documents getting lost in the office paperwork shuffle. For instance, some provide employees

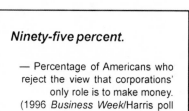

Ninety-five percent.

— Percentage of Americans who reject the view that corporations' only role is to make money. (1996 *Business Week*/Harris poll of 1,004 adult Americans)

framed copies for the office walls or have them printed on wallet cards, stationary or other items. At Perot Systems, former CEO Mort Meyerson says he routinely handed out laminated cards listing the company's values and "style." Among the elements: "lead by example," "create an atmosphere of mutual trust and respect" — even "have fun."

IDEA #35
Hold Creative Contests for Employees

Reward employees for their artistic flair. Offer prizes for creations that best illustrate some aspect of the company code of ethics. You'll not only remind employees of the company's stated values, but encourage the staff to think a little more about what the document means and whether or not the company is "walking its talk."

In announcing your contest, list an e-mail address, phone number or other means by which employees can share their thoughts about the code of ethics and related issues.

Organize a staff meeting — or even an awards ceremony — where you announce winners and display their works. Use this opportunity to talk seriously about the company's ethics code and how well the company is adhering to it.

IDEA #36

Sponsor Art/Essay Contests for Employees' Kids

As part of a contest for employees' children (or nieces, nephews, grandchildren or other young people), encourage staff members to talk to the kids about the importance of good character. Then hold a contest with prizes for those who best express the meaning of good character or a specific ethical value (e.g., one of the "Six Pillars of Character" — trustworthiness, respect, responsibility, fairness, caring and good citizenship).

Use this opportunity to get your organization involved with **CHARACTER COUNTS!** (www.charactercounts.org), the nation's most widely used character-education framework.

Example:

- As part of its annual "Integrity Week" — held in mid-October to coincide with National **CHARACTER COUNTS!** Week — AlliedSignal Aerospace in Torrance, California, holds an essay contest for its employees' children. The company also has sponsored an essay contest focusing on the Six Pillars of Character for the students at a nearby junior high school.

> *Say your father was umpiring your baseball game. You're up with the bases loaded and a full count. A home run could win it. The ball shaves the outside corner and the ump calls what he sees. That is total fairness.*
>
> — Sixth-grader Jesse Macleod, from his winning essay on the Six Pillars of Character (sponsored by AlliedSignal Aerospace)

Visit www.charactercounts.org to learn more about how your business can participate in **CHARACTER COUNTS!** *activities.*

IDEA #37
Display 'Table Tents' in the Lunchroom

Example:

• During its "Integrity Week" AlliedSignal Aerospace (see previous page) posed a new pair of ethical questions each day to employees. Placed on cafeteria tables in the lunchroom, "table tents" asked them to think about the meaning of integrity, one of the company's seven core values. A sample table tent:

Your boss forges his superior's signature in order to meet a deadline on a project. He says the superior has approved this. What do you do?

a. Nothing. (wrong)

b. Insist your supervisor call his superior. (weak)

c. Advise your boss to sign his own name as acting for the superior. (yes)

d. Keep quiet but later call the hotline anonymously. (OK, but cowardly)

Online Resources

The ideas in this book come from a variety of newspapers, magazines, books and websites. Consult the resources below to find more ideas for encouraging employees to behave ethically and for conducting a socially and environmentally responsible business:

- The BellSouth Office of Ethics and Compliance website (www.ethics.bellsouth.com) posts the company's values and code of conduct. Designed for employees, the site also provides suggestions on dealing with ethical issues, plus an online game with ethics scenarios.

- The Boston College Center for Corporate Citizenship website (www.bcccc.net) offers *Integration: Critical Link for Corporate Citizenship*, a 2005 report that chronicles and analyzes eight companies' corporate citizenship initiatives.

- *Business Ethics* magazine online (www.business-ethics.com) offers articles and publications for sale, including its useful booklets of "Working Ideas."

- BusinessEthics.ca, a Canadian website, posts articles, case studies and other resources. There are separate sites for professional ethics, science and technology ethics, and government ethics.

- The Conference Board (www.conference-board.org) presents research and information on business ethics and compliance.

- Co-op America's annual *National Green Pages: A Directory of Products and Services for People and the Planet* (www.coopamerica.org)

PART TWO

Effective Ethics Codes

Introduction: Ethics Codes Don't Make People Ethical
by Michael Josephson 57

Ten Benefits of Having an Ethics Code 58

Making the Code Effective 59

Starting With a Values Statement 60

What an Ethics Code Should Say 61

Interpreting Behavioral Regulations 70

Language 71

Part Two: Introduction
Ethics Codes Don't Make People Ethical

by Michael Josephson

In the wake of a continual parade of scandals, there has been a lot of talk concerning codes of ethics. I've written dozens of codes and have a healthy respect for their value as an element of a corporate culture, but I wince at the unreasonable expectations attached to these documents.

First of all, ethics codes don't make people ethical. They don't make bad people good. Nor do they make people with bad judgment wise. Most of the very bad behavior we've seen in recent years would not have been prevented by an ethics code.

You see, there are two aspects to ethics: discernment — knowing right from wrong — and discipline — having the moral will power to do what's right. A code can help define what's right and acceptable and provide a basis for imposing sanctions on those who don't follow it. But unless it reinforces an established ethical culture, it won't do much to assure that people do what's right.

It's proper and prudent to clarify obligations under existing laws and establish standards of conduct in areas not governed by law. In effect, ethics codes transform one perspective of a moral obligation into a binding rule. For example, it's helpful to set clear parameters for the use of e-mails, private information and company property, hiring or doing business with relatives, and the acceptance of gratuities. In more complex cases, codes can mandate disclosure or certification and forbid or restrict transactions such as loans and reimbursements that could create real or apparent conflicts of interest.

To the extent we need more clarity, we need more codes. To the extent we need more character, we need a lot more.

Los Angeles — March, 2005

Michael Josephson is founder and president of the Josephson Institute of Ethics in Los Angeles.

Ten Benefits of Having an Ethics Code

Companies should have ethics codes to promote ethical behavior — not to enhance productivity, profits or public relations. Still, a sound, well-administered code can benefit a company and its stakeholders in a variety of ways. It can:

1. Guide employees in situations where the ethical course of action is not immediately obvious.

2. Help the company reinforce — and acquaint new employees with — its culture and values. A code can help create a climate of integrity and excellence.

3. Help the company communicate its expectations to the staff and to suppliers, vendors and customers. Also, by soliciting feedback and questions, a company can use the code to encourage frequent, open and honest communication among employees.

4. Minimize subjective and inconsistent management standards. A code explicitly outlines the rights and responsibilities of staff members and helps guard against capricious and preferential treatment of employees.

5. Help a company remain in compliance with complex government regulations. The landmark Sarbanes-Oxley Act of 2002 requires public companies to have an ethics code for senior financial officers.

6. Build public trust and enhance business reputations. Also, a code helps demonstrate the company's values to socially responsible investors.

7. Offer protection in preempting or defending against lawsuits.

8. Enhance morale, employee pride, loyalty and the recruiting of outstanding employees.

9. Help promote constructive social change by raising awareness of the community's needs and encouraging employees and other stakeholders to help.

10. Promote market efficiency — especially in areas where laws are weak or inefficient — by rewarding the best and most ethical producers of goods and services.

Adapted from W. W. Manley's *Executive's Handbook of Model Business Conduct Codes* (Prentice Hall, 1991)

Making the Code Effective

Simply *having* an ethics code is not enough. In fact, many of the companies that made headlines for massive scandals had some kind of conduct code. Enron's was particularly long and elaborate.

An ethics code can help guide employees on the path to integrity, accountability and excellence. It provides a compass and guideposts, but much more is required to ensure that the path is clear and that everyone wants to stay on it.

The process of creating and disseminating the code is important. Then the company must demonstrate that it is committed to it — even when it entails great sacrifice. This begins with the CEO and other senior officers, who must consistently reinforce the company's values in word and deed.

> *You have to continually emphasize ethics. Employees are very perceptive. They see through hollow statements. You can be the most eloquent speaker, but if you are evasive in your everyday dealings, if you don't treat people well, if you don't keep expenses carefully, they'll follow your example.*
>
> — Col. Ernst Volgenau, founder of SRA International, a global technology consulting firm

Lisa H. Newton, director of the Program in Applied Ethics at Fairfield University, sums up the requirements of an effective ethics code:

1. In its *development and promulgation*, the code must enjoy the maximum participation of the company's officers and employees (the principle of *participation*);

2. In its *content*, the code must be congruent with general ethical principles and the dictates of conscience (the principle of *validity*);

3. In its *implementation*, the code must be, and must be seen to be, coherent with the lived commitments of the company's officers (the principle of *authenticity*).

From *Taking Sides: Clashing Views on Controversial Issues in Business Ethics and Society* (Dushkin, 1996)

Written as distinct documents or integrated into one guide, the best business ethics codes contain three elements:

1. *A Values Statement* (also known as a "Statement of Guiding Principles," "Vision Statement" or "Credo")

2. *A Code of Conduct* (guidelines of employee and company responsibilities for operating ethically)

3. *Guidelines on Legal Compliance* (with explanations of relevant legal provisions)

Starting With a Values Statement

If you are creating an original ethics code, start by involving all employees in drafting a values statement. This is the place for listing basic ideals and inspirational statements.

Be sure to include everyone in the company — from the copier room to the corner office. Even a superbly worded document may become a source of snickering, even cynicism, if employees feel that management is imposing a corporate belief system from on high. As one employee at Alltel Mobile Communications told *Fortune* magazine, "It is, in my view, a crock of s---. Not so much because of what's on the [Alltel Mobile Credo]. It's that the company is forcing this on you — they're throwing up all over you with their philosophy. I'm good at my job. . . . All I want to do is go out and do it, without some idiot in a leather chair telling me how to think."

Develop a List of Core Ethical Values

The process might start with senior management developing and distributing a list of core ethical and business values. Be sure to lay the foundation of the statement with *ethical* values. You might begin with the Six Pillars of Character: *trustworthiness, respect, responsibility, fairness, caring* and *citizenship*. Because these values transcend politics, culture and religion, the Josephson Institute uses them as the basis for its programs and materials. Many businesses — along with thousands of schools, human-service organizations and entire communities — have formally embraced the Six Pillars.

Get Employee Feedback on Operational Values

Next, solicit ideas from employees through interviews, focus groups and questionnaires. Ask them to characterize the company's current values (as revealed in management-employee relations; intra-departmental relations; the company's relations with suppliers, vendors and customers; and its treatment of the local community and the environment). Then ask what these values *should* be. Lastly, account for variation in opinion and put a few final versions to a vote by the whole staff.

> *A vision statement is like the sun. You can't ever get there, but it's an attractive force that stimulates the growth of many things.*
>
> — Greg Steltenpohl,
> co-chief executive of
> Odwalla, a maker of juices

What an Ethics Code Should Say

An ethical code of conduct must arise naturally from the company's stated values and should provide detailed guidance for handling ethical challenges. General principles without specific provisions risk being perceived by employees as just so much window dressing. This may breed cynicism rather than commitment. What follows are some tips on what to say and how to say it.

Make It Specific

Start each section of the code by invoking the company's stated values on a given issue (often a line can come directly from the company's values statement). Next, state guidelines and examples of how the principle applies in specific, realistic situations. For example, with respect to environmental responsibilities, Coca-Cola's "Code of Business Conduct" reads:

> The Company's highest priority is protecting the safety and health of our employees, customers and members of the communities where we do business. In addition, we are committed to waste recycling programs and conservation methods. The Company recognizes its responsibility for protection of human health, the environment and natural resources. You

[a Coca-Cola employee] are responsible for performing your job functions in accordance with the Company's environmental policies. . . . You must respond promptly and professionally, in accordance with applicable procedures, to any potential threat to human health or the environment.

Make It Comprehensive

Though its provisions must be specific and clear, an ethics code should cover a lot of ground. At a minimum, it should address the Six Pillars of Character: trustworthiness, respect, responsibility, fairness, caring and citizenship. (A sampling of statements from company codes on additional topics follows this section.)

Trustworthiness: Safeguard public confidence in the integrity of the organization by displaying honesty in all dealings and avoiding conduct that might create the appearance of impropriety. Go beyond what is legally required to permit public scrutiny of your activities. Examples:

- *The goal of corporate communication is the truth — well and persuasively told. In our advertising and other public communications, we will avoid not only untruths, but also exaggeration and overstatement.* (Caterpillar, Inc., "A Code of Worldwide Business Conduct and Operating Principles")

- *Our business is based on a strong tradition of trust. It is the reason our customers come to us. Honesty and integrity are cornerstones of ethical behavior — and trustworthiness and dependability are essential to lasting relationships. Our continued success depends on doing what we promise — promptly, competently and fairly.* ("American Express Company Code of Conduct")

Respect: Treat others with dignity — the way you would like to be treated. Be civil, courteous and decent with all employees, customers and business partners. Example:

- *We will consistently treat customers and company resources with the respect they deserve. . . . We treat one another with respect and take pride in the significant contributions that come from the diversity of individuals and ideas. . . . We owe our suppliers the same type of respect that we show to our customers.*

("Northrop Grumman Values")

Responsibility: Conduct business efficiently and honorably in a manner that permits employees, suppliers, vendors, customers and members of the local community to make informed judgments and hold the company accountable. Example:

- *We accept individual responsibility, in partnership with the company, for the success of the business, for our personal development and for balancing work and family responsibilities.* ("The Chevron Way")

Fairness: Seek to be impartial; employ independent objective judgment on merit, free from conflicts of interest — both real and apparent. Compensate all employees equitably; minimize wage disparities. Examples:

- *Wherever it operates in the world, the corporation offers salaries and benefits that are competitive and fair. . . . In its hiring practices, Nortel will be fair and equitable.* (Northern Telecom, "Commitments to Nortel Stakeholders")

- *The BagelWorks wage ratio ensures that the highest salary is only 3.5 times more than the lowest.* (BagelWorks)

> **Many companies state their values in employee handbooks (71 percent), list them in company brochures (67 percent) and post them on their websites (50 percent).**
>
> — Corporate Values Survey, American Management Association, 2002

Caring: Demonstrate a genuine sense of compassion and concern for the welfare of others — inside and outside the company walls. Don't allow tax advantages to dictate charitable contributions from the company. These are ploys, not contributions.

Citizenship: Honor and respect the principles and spirit of democracy and set a positive example by observing the letter and spirit of laws. Demonstrate a commitment to the environment and to social responsibility that goes beyond legal requirements. Example:

- *Our social mission . . . is to operate the company in a way that actively recognizes the central role that business plays in the structure of society by initiating innovative ways to improve the quality of life of a broad community: local, national and international.* (Ben & Jerry's)

Provide Commentary With Explanations and Illustrations

Include commentary that helps explain the underlying rationale of the code and provide a range of practical common applications. Although no code can foresee and address every situation, it should anticipate questions employees might have in certain scenarios. A common format is the hypothetical Q&A. Coca-Cola's code uses this structure:

Q: What should I do if I know or suspect that an environmental violation is occurring at my facility?

A: You need to bring your concern to the attention of your supervisor or facility management. If the issue cannot be resolved with local management, take the issue to divisional or regional management, or if you wish to discuss it confidentially or anonymously, call the Hotline at [toll-free number]. In no event will the Company take any action against you for making a complaint or disclosing information in good faith. You will not lose your job for reporting potential environmental violations which you reasonably believe may have occurred, and any retaliation against you is prohibited.

Sears and Roebuck Company peppers the margins of its Code of Business Conduct with Q&A's. Some examples:

Q: While ringing up a sale recently, I noticed that an item was mismarked and the customer was being overcharged. The customer did not seem to notice, and there were many people waiting in line. Would it be alright not to mention the error?

A: No, it is never acceptable to overcharge a customer. Charge the customer the correct price and advise your manager that the item is mismarked.

Q: A stockbroker has suggested an investment in a new company. Although I am not directly involved, I am aware of confidential negotiations that might result in that company becoming a significant Sears source. May I follow the stockbroker's advice?

A: No. Since you have some knowledge of these confidential negotiations, following the stockbroker's advice might be considered prohibited insider trading.

Q: May my spouse accompany me on a vendor sponsored business trip?

A: Yes, provided you family or Sears pays for your spouse's expenses. You may not accept hospitality for your spouse from an existing or prospective supplier.

Q: If I give a small payment to a customs official, I can bring back samples from my buying trips much more easily. The law calls these "facilitating" payments and allows them. Can I make these payments in order to make my job easier?

A: No. Sears follows a higher standard. Payments to government officials or agents, no matter their size or purpose, are not allowed.

Provide General Decision-Making Tips

A code of ethics should not be designed to have employees memorize what kind of behavior is proper in certain situations. It should teach good judgment and illustrate how good choices are made.

The Molson Coors Brewing Co., with a comprehensive ethics program that *Workforce Management* magazine called a model, seeks to do this with its ethics code — and with interactive online courses, ethics leadership training and other resources that support the code. Says Warren Malmquist, who developed the program and serves as director of Coors Audit Services: "The goal of the program is to step beyond rules and guidelines and teach employees how to think, clarify and analyze situations."

The American Express Company Code of Conduct is another good example. It suggests employees ask themselves:

- Am I compromising my own personal ethics in any way?

- Would I like to see my action become a general industry practice?

- How would I feel if my action were reported on the front page of my local newspaper?

- Would the Company lose customers — or shareholders — if they knew employees did this?

- Would I be comfortable explaining my action to my spouse? My parents? My children?

See *"Clarify the Code of Conduct"* on page 9 to read how the Arizona Public Service Company handles questions about its ethics code.

Make It Clear and Unambiguous

Pedantic jargon is a sure sign of a poorly written code, but vague terms and platitudes are just as bad. Absent some guidance as to their interpretation, phrases such as "improper use" and "undue personal benefits" are of little help and may be confusing. Be sure that all parts of the code (the values statement, standards and guidelines, specific rules and definitions) are clear and unambiguous. To accomplish this:

- Use direct and simple language, defining any term or phrase whose meaning may not be self-evident to the average reader.

- Be careful with terms that indicate whether the provision is mandatory and enforceable (e.g., "shall," "must") or simply aspirational or advisory (e.g., "should").

- Do not use the same terminology at different times to mean different things.

- Make liberal use of examples and illustrations to clarify the principle or rule.

- Use action verbs; avoid the passive voice.

Make It Easy to Read and Use

General Electric's code of conduct is so detailed and complex that the designers wrote a user's guide to help the reader wade through its provisions. The subject of ethics in the workplace is daunting enough for most employees; don't make your code of ethics more intimidating than it has to be. Use these tips to make it as accessible as possible:

- Avoid opaque cross-references to code section numbers, or worse, to other materials (such as government regulations) not included in the code (e.g., "As provided by section 56.897(a) . . ." or "Additional limitations are imposed by 56 U.S.C. 18763."). It is better to paraphrase relevant references so that each provision is essentially self-contained. Similarly, include definitions in appropriate provisions rather than hiding them in another section of the code.

- Typeset the document so that it is easily readable. Typefaces should generally be at least 11-point or above in size (never less than 10-point). Consider using wide margins with summaries, breakout quotes, caption headings or double-columning to improve readability.

- Edit and proofread for typographical errors, poor grammar and misspellings. What kind of message are you sending if you can't be bothered to correctly spell the company's values? (In researching numerous company ethics codes, we found several riddled with errors.)

> *We realized that it was essential to develop a code of ethics that is meaningful, rather than a legal-based document that's difficult to understand.*
>
> — Caroline McMichen, group manager of ethics and audit services at Molson Coors Brewing Co.

- Include a detailed table of contents and a functionally designed index (using words readers are likely to recognize).

- Many companies have found it effective to use one-page summaries, special websites, wallet cards, posters and other innovative presentation techniques. But don't get too carried away. Ben & Jerry's may have stayed within the bounds of reason when they reportedly put their values statement on a cube, but, as *Fortune* noted in 1993, some companies seem to be pushing the envelope:

  > PSE&G's electric business unit [has] created a values-based shaving kit. The kit contains a pen and a set of disposable razors. Each razor is emblazoned on its back with one of the six Core Values. Shave with one, for example, and you are reminded that

PSE&G stands for 'lean, cost-effective operations'; with another, 'teamwork and collaboration.' The pen has a transparent window, the kind that in naughty pens shows a woman disrobing. Every time its button is depressed, a new value, such as 'corporate citizenship,' pops into view.

Keep It Short and Simple

The entire U.S. Constitution is shorter than many business codes of ethics. Make an effort to avoid complex provisions and sentences that contain more than one requirement or exception. Generally, list and enumerate multiple requirements for easy reference and to assure that the reader knows each point is a distinct one. Draw up bullet-pointed lists rather than stringing out multifaceted ideas in long sentences with commas and semicolons.

Be Realistic

Do not impose standards of conduct that are either too difficult to adhere to (e.g., "absolutely no personal phone calls") or too difficult to interpret and apply (leading to such questions as "Does 'accept no gifts or gratuities' mean I must decline a cup of coffee when I'm at the distributor's office?").

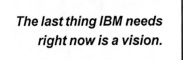

The last thing IBM needs right now is a vision.

— CEO Louis V. Gerstner Jr.'s irate response to a reporter in 1993, after the company announced $8.9 billion in cutbacks

Be Sure It's Enforceable

Be certain the provisions are enforceable in terms of union agreements, other regulations and Constitutional rights. In addition, be sure there is a mechanism for enforcement and that the resources are available to enforce the code. A credible and efficient process for receiving complaints, investigating charges and determining guilt or innocence is crucial.

Periodically Challenge It

As part of a continuing program of ethics awareness and education, periodically put your company values statement and code of ethical conduct to the test. An honest, candid, even highly self-critical assessment of operational values versus stated values is itself a good way to teach integrity by example.

Although Johnson & Johnson has made a number of minor amendments to its Credo over the years, business ethics textbooks often cite the effectiveness of the 1975 "Credo Challenge Meetings" at which then-president James Burke assembled senior managers from several countries. Mr. Burke reportedly began the series of discussions by noting that this document was displayed in offices around the world, but if the managers in attendance were not personally committed to it, then it was "an act of pretention and should be ripped off the walls."

Make It Clear That the Code Applies Abroad and at Home

As business becomes increasingly globalized, specific guidelines for doing business in foreign cultures have become more necessary. Without an explicit ethical code of conduct, many employees abroad may find themselves lost in what seem to be ethically ambiguous situations. Thomas Donaldson, a professor of business ethics at the University of Pennsylvania's Wharton School, says that ethics codes should stress three cross-cultural values:

> *Respect for Human Dignity*: Create and sustain a culture in which employees, customers and suppliers are treated not as means to an end but as people whose intrinsic value must be acknowledged. Produce safe products and services in a safe workplace.

> *Respect for Basic Rights*: Act in ways that support and protect the individual rights of employees, customers, and surrounding communities. Avoid relationships that violate human beings' rights to health, education, safety and an adequate standard of living.

> *Good Citizenship*: Support essential social institutions, such as the economic system and the education system. Work with host governments and other institutions to protect the environment.

Employees should have no doubts about their code's validity when conducting business on foreign soil. Federal law (the Foreign Corrupt Practices Act of 1977) imposes criminal penalties on American enterprises that bribe officials of foreign governments.

In March of 1996, the Paris-based International Chamber of Commerce released a report on "Extortion and Bribery in International Business Transactions," recommending that:

[E]nterprises should, where appropriate, draw up their own codes consistent with the ICC Rules and apply them to the particular circumstances in which their business is carried out. Such codes may usefully include examples and should enjoin employees or agents who find themselves subjected to any form of extortion or bribery immediately to report the same to senior corporate management. Companies should develop clear policies, guidelines, and training programs for implementing and enforcing the provisions of their codes.

The U.S. Alien Tort Claims Act of 1789 also holds American corporations responsible for their conduct abroad. In 2005, Unocal Corp. settled a landmark human rights lawsuit that claimed it was responsible for forced labor, rapes and a murder allegedly carried out by soldiers along a pipeline project in Myanmar (formerly Burma). The suit was filed on behalf of Burmese citizens under the U.S. Alien Tort Claims Act.

Most Importantly, Practice the Preaching

One of the greatest sources of employee cynicism and demoralization is the flouting of stated ethical rules and obligations by senior management. Establishing an ethical culture in the workplace is a process, not an end. That process requires the company's leaders to set an example by demonstrating the highest levels of integrity and accountability. This means not just telling the truth when there is little to gain from lying, for instance, but doing the right thing even when it costs more than you think you can afford to pay.

An ethics code can be a vital moral road map . . . or self-congratulatory bombast. What gives it value is not its prose, but the commitment of those who tend to its implementation.

Interpreting Behavioral Regulations

All regulations — whether criminal laws, government rules, agency standards of conduct or office policies — have to affect behavior or they are pointless. They come in several forms:

1. *Prohibitions.* The most common kind of regulation forbids or restricts conduct (e.g., acceptance of gifts, outside income, post-employment activities, retaliation).

2. ***Mandates.*** Less frequently, regulations require certain conduct (e.g., reporting waste, fraud or abuse; safeguarding government assets).

3. ***Procedures.*** Some regulations outline procedures to be followed to assure integrity, accountability, or order (e.g., financial disclosure, written permission for outside income).

4. ***Aspirational.*** A final group of regulations seeks to encourage behavior that is not formally required (e.g., making an honest effort).

Language

1. ***Legalistic.*** Terms such as "shall" or "shall not," "must" or "must not," and "may" or "may not" indicate mandates and prohibitions. Carefully define any regulations that use these terms so they can be fairly and consistently enforced. Failure to enforce mandatory provisions deals a blow to all company policies. Therefore, standards should not be expressed in legalistic, mandatory language unless there is a firm intention and clear ability to enforce the requirements.

2. ***Ethical (aspirational):*** Terms like "should," "ought," and "proper" or "improper" are often used in very different ways. In some cases, as with standards of conduct and office policies, they take on the character of mandatory legal provisions using "shall" or "shall not." If employees do things that are "improper" or that they "should not" do — or if they fail to do what is "proper" or what they "should" do — they might be subject to discipline, even termination. On the other hand, these terms may simply express moral goals and exhortations to live up to high ethical standards. When used this way, there is no intent to enforce the provisions. Such ambiguity undermines a code of conduct, as the reader cannot distinguish between mandatory and aspirational provisions. Therefore, it is best to use terms like "shall" and "must" when enforceability is intended. Again, make every effort to avoid ambiguity so that employees know what is expected of them.

3. ***Permissive (discretionary):*** Some provisions clarify ambiguous requirements (e.g., the duty to avoid appearances of impropriety or the obligation to avoid conflicts of interest) and limit the scope of

previous prohibitions by specifying behavior that is permitted but not necessarily encouraged (e.g., the right to accept gifts worth less than $25). Such provisions might include the terms "may" or "is not prohibited." "Permissible" conduct may be simply a lesser form of prohibited conduct. It may be deemed permissible because it is too difficult to detect or enforce.

Such conduct is not ethical simply because it is allowed. Generally, the test is the "spirit" of the rule: Does the permissible act create problems of actual or apparent impropriety? Standards of conduct should explicitly address this point to assure that employees operating in good faith understand that they should do more than they are formally required and less than they are technically allowed.

APPENDIX

Sample Ethics Codes and Documents

A Letter to Employees from the Head of the Company 75

Corporate Values Statement ("Our Credo," Johnson & Johnson) 77

Environmental Values Statement ("Environmental Mission Statement,"
    Starbucks Coffee Company) 79

Guidelines for Doing Business Abroad ("Global Sourcing and Operating
    Guidelines," Levi Strauss & Company) 80

Whistleblower Protections ("Retaliation Against Informants,"
    Sarbanes-Oxley Act, 2002) 84

Guidelines for Whistleblowing ("Responsibility and Consequences,"
    Northrop Grumman's "Standards of Business Conduct") 85

Model Code for Business ("The Caux Round Table Principles
    for Business") 86

Compiled Ethics Codes: A Sampling of Topics 94

Resources on Ethics Codes 110

A Letter to Employees From the Head of the Company

A letter from the company CEO often precedes a values statement and code of ethical conduct. This letter should stress that the code is meant to assure the highest respect for members of the company. It should in no way imply that employees are predisposed to misconduct. Yet it should be clear that the company has high expectations of employees. For example:

An enduring set of values is fundamental to the way in which we conduct our business at Sears, Roebuck and Co. Sears associates are expected to deal honestly, responsibly and fairly with everyone with whom we do business.

These are not new ideas at Sears, but it is vital that each and every associate make a personal commitment to uphold them. We must each work hard to achieve the highest standards of ethical business conduct — "the high road" — and to further the bond of trust we enjoy with our customers, suppliers, investors, government officials and fellow associates. . . .

. . . "Our Shared Beliefs," "Leadership Principles," and "Code of Business Conduct" provide you with a sound base for your decision making responsibilities. I request that you then take personal responsibility for your unit, your customers, and your decisions and, as appropriate, transfer responsibility to your colleagues. . . .

Arthur C. Martinez, Chairman and CEO
Sears, Roebuck and Co., 1995

A Letter to Employees From the Head of the Company

The letter might also mention examples of how the company demonstrates its values:

> *. . . The easy part of describing our vision of caring capitalism to the world was to hold forth a picture of how commerce might be an innovative source of creative social problem-solving energy as well as an attractive source of profit. . . . The growing PartnerShop program, under which not-for-profit organizations own and manage ice cream scoop shops, is developing some successful models of uniting business and social concerns into one enterprise. . . . We have undertaken supplier relationships with companies [that are] fulfilling laudable commitments to [their] communities for providing work careers, job training, affordable housing, and child care programs. . . . These and many other supplier relationships and commitments are important to us because they advance our vision of how food should be produced and of how businesses can expand their social commitments in their communities. . . .*

Bob Holland, CEO
Ben & Jerry's Homemade, Inc.

If there have been ethical lapses, they should not be glossed over. In fact, a letter from the president or CEO should exhibit a good deal of candor in this regard. In "Integrity: Three Hughes Case Histories — What Went Wrong, Why It Went Wrong, and Lessons Learned," the company chairman concludes his letter to employees by saying:

> *The three case histories presented in this booklet are lessons from which we all can learn. They highlight what can go wrong when management fails in its responsibilities.*
>
> *I hope we have no more examples to share with you in the future.*

C. Michael Armstrong
Chairman and CEO, Hughes

Corporate Values Statement

"Our Credo"
(Johnson & Johnson)

*We believe our first responsibility is to the
doctors, nurses and patients,
to mothers and fathers and all others who
use our products and services.
In meeting their needs everything we do must be of high quality.
We must constantly strive to reduce our costs
in order to maintain reasonable prices.
Customers' orders must be serviced promptly and accurately.
Our suppliers and distributors must have an opportunity
to make a fair profit.*

*We are responsible to our employees,
the men and women who work with us throughout the world.
Everyone must be considered as an individual.
We must respect their dignity and recognize their merit.
They must have a sense of security in their jobs.
Compensation must be fair and adequate,
and working conditions clean, orderly and safe.
We must be mindful of ways to help our employees fulfill
their family responsibilities.
Employees must feel free to make suggestions and complaints.
There must be equal opportunity for employment,
development and advancement for those qualified.
We must provide competent management,
and their actions must be just and ethical.*

*We are responsible to the communities in which we live and work
and to the world community as well.
We must be good citizens — support good works and charities
and bear our fair share of taxes.
We must encourage civic improvements and
better health and education.*

"Our Credo," cont.
(Johnson & Johnson)

We must maintain in good order
the property we are privileged to use,
protecting the environment and natural resources.

Our final responsibility is to our stockholders.
Business must make a sound profit.
We must experiment with new ideas.
Research must be carried on, innovative programs developed
and mistakes paid for.
New equipment must be purchased, new facilities provided
and new products launched.
Reserves must be created to provide for adverse times.
When we operate according to these principles,
the stockholders should realize a fair return.

Environmental Values Statement

"Environmental Mission Statement"
(Starbucks Coffee Company)

*Starbucks is committed to a role of
environmental leadership in all facets of our business.*

We will fulfill this mission by a commitment to:

*Understanding of environmental issues
and sharing information with our partners.*

*Developing innovative and flexible
solutions to bring about change.*

*Striving to buy, sell and use
environmentally friendly products.*

*Instilling environmental responsibility
as a corporate value.*

*Measuring and monitoring
our progress for each project.*

*Encouraging all partners
to share in our mission.*

Guidelines for Doing Business Abroad

"Global Sourcing and Operating Guidelines"
(Levi Strauss & Company)

Our Global Sourcing and Operating Guidelines help us to select business partners who follow workplace standards and business practices that are consistent with our company's values. These requirements are applied to every contractor who manufactures or finishes products for Levi Strauss & Co. Trained inspectors closely audit and monitor compliance among approximately 600 cutting, sewing, and finishing contractors in more than 60 countries.

The Levi Strauss & Co. Global Sourcing and Operating Guidelines include two parts:

I. **The Country Assessment Guidelines**, which address large, external issues beyond the control of Levi Strauss & Co.'s individual business partners. These help us assess the opportunities and risks of doing business in a particular country.

II. **The Business Partner Terms of Engagement**, which deal with issues that are substantially controllable by individual business partners. These Terms of Engagement are an integral part of our business relationships. Our employees and our business partners understand that complying with our Terms of Engagement is no less important than meeting our quality standards or delivery times.

Country Assessment Guidelines

The numerous countries where Levi Strauss & Co. has existing or future business interests present a variety of cultural, political, social and economic circumstances.

The Country Assessment Guidelines help us assess any issue that might present concern in light of the ethical principles we have set for ourselves. The Guidelines assist us in making practical and principled business decisions as we balance the potential risks and opportunities associated with conducting business in specific countries. Specifically, we assess whether the:

"Global Sourcing and Operating Guidelines," cont.
(Levi Strauss & Company)

• **Health and Safety Conditions** would meet the expectations we have for employees and their families or our company representatives;

• **Human Rights Environment** would allow us to conduct business activities in a manner that is consistent with our Global Sourcing and Operating Guidelines and other company policies;

• **Legal System** would provide the necessary support to adequately protect our trademarks, investments or other commercial interests, or to implement the Global Sourcing and Operating Guidelines and other company policies; and

• **Political, Economic and Social Environment** would protect the company's commercial interests and brand/corporate image. We will not conduct business in countries prohibited by U.S. laws.

Terms of Engagement

• **Ethical Standards**

We will seek to identify and utilize business partners who aspire as individuals and in the conduct of all their businesses to a set of ethical standards not incompatible with our own.

• **Legal Requirements**

We expect our business partners to be law abiding as individuals and to comply with legal requirements relevant to the conduct of all their businesses.

• **Environmental Requirements**

We will only do business with partners who share our commitment to the environment and who conduct their business in a way that is consistent with Levi Strauss & Co.'s Environmental Philosophy and Guiding Principles.

Guidelines for Doing Business Abroad

"Global Sourcing and Operating Guidelines," cont.
(Levi Strauss & Company)

- **Community Involvement**

We will favor business partners who share our commitment to improving community conditions.

- **Employment Standards**

We will only do business with partners who adhere to the following guidelines:

Child Labor: Use of child labor is not permissible. Workers can be no less than 15 years of age and not younger than the compulsory age to be in school. We will not utilize partners who use child labor in any of their facilities. We support the development of legitimate workplace apprenticeship programs for the educational benefit of younger people.

Prison Labor/Forced Labor: We will not utilize prison or forced labor in contracting relationships in the manufacture and finishing of our products. We will not utilize or purchase materials from a business partner utilizing prison or forced labor.

Disciplinary Practices: We will not utilize business partners who use corporal punishment or other forms of mental or physical coercion.

Working Hours: While permitting flexibility in scheduling, we will identify local legal limits on work hours and seek business partners who do not exceed them except for appropriately compensated overtime. While we favor partners who utilize less than sixty-hour workweeks, we will not use contractors who, on a regular basis, require in excess of a sixty-hour week. Employees should be allowed at least one day off in seven.

Guidelines for Doing Business Abroad

"Global Sourcing and Operating Guidelines," cont.
(Levi Strauss & Company)

Wages and Benefits: We will only do business with partners who provide wages and benefits that comply with any applicable law and match the prevailing local manufacturing or finishing industry practices.

Freedom of Association: We respect workers' rights to form and join organizations of their choice and to bargain collectively. We expect our suppliers to respect the right to free association and the right to organize and bargain collectively without unlawful interference. Business partners should ensure that workers who make such decisions or participate in such organizations are not the object of discrimination or punitive disciplinary actions and that the representatives of such organizations have access to their members under conditions established either by local laws or mutual agreement between the employer and the worker organizations.

Discrimination: While we recognize and respect cultural differences, we believe that workers should be employed on the basis of their ability to do the job, rather than on the basis of personal characteristics or beliefs. We will favor business partners who share this value.

Health & Safety: We will only utilize business partners who provide workers with a safe and healthy work environment. Business partners who provide residential facilities for their workers must provide safe and healthy facilities.

Whistleblower Protections

"Retaliation Against Informants"
(From the Sarbanes-Oxley Act, 2002)

Editor's note: The federal Sarbanes-Oxley Act of 2002 strengthens whistleblower protections and specifies criminal penalties for retaliating against those who report wrongdoing. Many codes now provide guidelines for reporting suspected violations.

> **Sarbanes-Oxley Criminal Provision,**
> **18 USC § 1107. Retaliation Against Informants.**
> Whoever knowingly, with the intent to retaliate, takes any action harmful to any person, including interference with the lawful employment or livelihood of any person, for providing to a law enforcement officer any truthful information relating to the commission or possible commission of any Federal offense, shall be fined under this title or imprisoned not more than 10 years, or both.

Guidelines for Whistleblowing

"Responsibility and Consequences"
(From Northrop Grumman's
"Standards of Business Conduct")

1) Responsibility: In addition to the Chief Executive Officer, the Chief Financial Officer and all other managers and employees, the Northrop Grumman Values and Standards of Business Conduct apply to members of the Board of Directors, consultants, agents, contract labor (job shoppers) and anyone who represents the company in any capacity. It is the responsibility of all of these parties to comply with the standards, to seek advice and guidance when questions arise and to report violations of the Standards of Business Conduct of which they have knowledge. Employees are encouraged to raise such issues with their manager first. In the event that is not possible, contact the local Business Conduct Officer, legal counsel, human resources or the Corporate or sector OpenLine. The company will treat such reports as confidential. You may make an anonymous report if you desire. In any case, company policy prohibits direct or indirect retaliation on anyone reporting a violation of the Standards of Business Conduct.

2) Consequences: Employees who violate company standards of conduct, especially those relating to our relationships with the U.S. Government but also those related to commercial customers, will be subject to disciplinary action up to and including termination of employment. Violations may also result in civil or criminal penalties. An employee who witnesses such a violation and fails to report it may be subject to discipline. Also, a supervisor or manager may be subject to discipline to the extent that the violation reflects inadequate supervision or lack of diligence.

Model Code for Business

"The Caux Round Table Principles for Business"

Editor's note: In 1994 a distinguished group of business leaders convened to develop a global standard for ethical business behavior. They produced the CRT Principles for Business, available in a dozen languages at www.cauxroundtable.org/principles.html.

Introduction

The principles of this code are rooted in two basic ethical ideals: kyosei *and human dignity. The Japanese concept of* kyosei *means living and working together for the common good — enabling cooperation and mutual prosperity to coexist with healthy and fair competition. "Human dignity" refers to the sacredness or value of each person as an end, not simply as a means to the fulfillment of another's purposes.*

The General Principles in Section 2 seek to clarify the spirit of kyosei *and "human dignity" while the specific Stakeholder Principles in Section 3 are concerned with their practical application.*

Section 1. Preamble
Section 2. General Principles
Section 3. Stakeholder Principles

SECTION 1. PREAMBLE

The mobility of employment, capital, produce and technology is making business increasingly global in its transactions and its effects.

Laws and market forces are necessary but insufficient guides for conduct.

Model Code for Business

"The Caux Round Table Principles for Business," cont.

Responsibility for the politics and actions of business and respect for the dignity and interests of its stakeholders are fundamental.

Shared values, including a commitment to shared prosperity, are as important for a global community as for communities of smaller scale.

For these reasons, and because business can be a powerful agent of positive social change, we offer the following principles as a foundation for dialogue and action by business leaders in search of business responsibility. In so doing, we affirm the necessity for moral values in business decision making. Without them, stable business relationships and a sustainable world community are impossible.

SECTION 2. GENERAL PRINCIPLES

Principle 1. The Responsibilities of Businesses: Beyond Shareholders Toward Stakeholders

The value of a business to society is the wealth and employment it creates and the marketable products and practices it provides to consumers at a reasonable price commensurate with quality. To create such value, a business must maintain its own economic health and viability, but survival is not a sufficient goal.

Businesses have a role to play in improving the lives of all their customers, employees and shareholders by sharing with them the wealth they have created. Suppliers and competitors as well should expect businesses to honor their obligations in a spirit of honesty and fairness. As responsible citizens of the local, national, regional, and global communities in which they operate, businesses share a part in shaping the future of those communities.

Model Code for Business

"The Caux Round Table Principles for Business," cont.

Principle 2. The Economic and Social Impact of Businesses: Toward Innovation, Justice and World Community

Businesses established in foreign countries to develop, produce or sell should also contribute to the social advancement of those countries by creating productive employment and helping to raise the purchasing power of their citizens. Businesses also should contribute to human rights, education, welfare, and vitalization of the countries in which they operate. Businesses should contribute to economic and social development not only in the countries in which they operate, but in the world community at large, through effective and prudent use of resources, free and fair competition and emphasis upon innovation in technology, production methods, marketing and communications.

Principle 3. Business Behavior: Beyond the Letter of Law Toward a Spirit of Trust

While accepting the legitimacy of trade secrets, businesses should recognize that sincerity, keeping of promises and transparency contribute not only to their own credibility and stability but also to the smoothness and efficiency of business transactions, particularly on the international level.

Principle 4. Respect for the Rules

To avoid trade frictions and to promote freer trade, equal conditions for competition, and fair and equitable treatment for all participants, businesses should respect international and domestic rules. In addition, they should recognize that some behavior, though legal, may still have adverse consequences.

Model Code for Business

"The Caux Round Table Principles for Business," cont.

Principle 5. Support for Multilateral Trade

Businesses should support the multilateral trade systems of GATT, the World Trade Organization and similar international agreements. They should cooperate in efforts to promote the progressive and judicious liberalization of trade, and to relax those domestic measures that unreasonably hinder global commerce, while giving due respect to national policy objectives.

Principle 6. Respect for the Environment

A business should protect and, where possible, improve the environment, promote sustainable development, and prevent the wasteful use of natural resources.

Principle 7. Avoidance of Illicit Operations

A business should not participate in or condone bribery, money laundering, or other corrupt practices. Indeed, it should seek cooperation with others to eliminate them. It should not trade in arms or other materials used for terrorist activities, drug traffic or other organized crime.

SECTION 3. STAKEHOLDER PRINCIPLES

Customers

We believe in treating all customers with dignity irrespective of whether they purchase our products and services directly from us or otherwise acquire them in the market. We therefore have a responsibility to:

*   provide our customers with the highest quality products and services consistent with their requirements

Model Code for Business

"The Caux Round Table Principles for Business," cont.

- treat our customers fairly in all aspects of our business transactions including a high level of service and remedies for their dissatisfaction

- make every effort to ensure that the health and safety of our customers, as well as the quality of their environment, will be sustained or enhanced by our products and services

- assure respect for human dignity in products offered, marketing, and advertising

- respect the integrity of the culture of our customers.

Employees

We believe in the dignity of every employee and in taking employee interests seriously. We therefore have a responsibility to:

- provide jobs and compensation that improve workers' living conditions

- provide working conditions that respect each employee's health and dignity

- be honest in communications with employees and open in sharing information, limited only by legal and competitive restraints

- listen to and, where possible, act on employee suggestions, ideas, requests, and complaints

- engage in good-faith negotiations when conflict arises

- avoid discriminatory practices and guarantee equal treatment and opportunity in areas such as gender, age, race, and religion

- promote in the business itself the employment of differently-abled people in places of work where they can be genuinely useful

Model Code for Business

"The Caux Round Table Principles for Business," cont.

- protect employees from avoidable injury and illness in the workplace

- encourage and assist employees in developing relevant and transferable skills and knowledge

- be sensitive to serious unemployment problems frequently associated with business decisions, and work with governments, employee groups, other agencies and each other in addressing these dislocations.

Owners/Investors

We believe in honoring the trust our investors place in us. We therefore have a responsibility to:

- apply professional and diligent management in order to secure a fair and competitive return on our owners' investment

- disclose relevant information to owners/investors subject only to legal requirements and competitive constraints

- conserve, protect, and increase the owner/investors' assets

- respect the owner/investors' requests, suggestions, complaints, and formal resolutions.

Suppliers

Our relationship with suppliers and subcontractors must be based on mutual respect. We therefore have a responsibility to:

- seek fairness and truthfulness in all of our activities, including pricing, licensing, and rights to sell

- ensure that our business activities are free from coercion and unnecessary litigation

Model Code for Business

"The Caux Round Table Principles for Business," cont.

- foster long-term stability in the supplier relationship in return for value, quality, competitiveness and reliability

- share information with suppliers and integrate them into our planning processes

- pay suppliers on time and in accordance with agreed terms of trade

- seek, encourage, and prefer suppliers and subcontractors whose employment practices respect human dignity.

Competitors

We believe that fair economic competition is one of the basic requirements for increasing the wealth of nations and ultimately for making possible the just distribution of goods and services. We therefore have a responsibility to:

- foster open markets for trade and investment

- promote competitive behavior that is socially and environmentally beneficial and demonstrates mutual respect among competitors

- refrain from either seeking or participating in questionable payments or favors to secure competitive advantages

- respect both tangible and intellectual property rights

- refuse to acquire commercial information by dishonest or unethical means, such as industrial espionage.

Communities

We believe that as global corporate citizens, we can contribute to

"The Caux Round Table
Principles for Business," cont.

such forces of reform and human rights as are at work in the communities which we open to. We therefore have a responsibility in those communities to:

- respect human rights and democratic institutions, and promote them wherever practicable

- recognize government's legitimate obligation to the society at large and support public policies and practices that promote human development through harmonious relations between business and other segments of society

- collaborate with those forces in the community dedicated to raising standards of health, education, workplace safety and economic well-being

- promote and stimulate sustainable development and play a leading role in preserving and enhancing the physical environment and conserving the earth's resources

- support peace, security, diversity and social integration

- respect the integrity of local cultures

- be a good corporate citizen through charitable donations, educational and cultural contributions and employee participation in community and civic affairs.

Compiled Ethics Codes:
A Sampling of Topics

Customer Relations

- We believe our first responsibility is to the doctors, nurses, and patients, to mothers and fathers and all others who use our products and services. In meeting their needs everything we do must be of high quality. Customers' orders must be serviced promptly and accurately. (Johnson & Johnson, "Our Credo")

- We seek to build sustained, comprehensive relationships with our customers and recognize the importance of continuity of the people and priorities that Citicorp brings to these relationships, and our consistency of purpose and presence. We are committed to quality and constantly strive to meet and exceed customer expectations. (Citibank, "Code of Conduct and Ethical Policies")

- We are dedicated to satisfying our customers. We believe in respecting our customers, listening to their requests and understanding their expectations. We strive to exceed their expectations in affordability, quality and on-time delivery. ("Northrop Grumman Values")

- We're honest with our customers. No deals, no bribes, no kickbacks, no secrets, no fooling around with prices. No promising something we can't deliver. Everything we offer is honestly made, truthfully represented, ethically sold. (Xerox, "An Understanding")

- Information disclosed by a customer to a Motorola employee and clearly identified verbally or in writing as sensitive, private or confidential shall be protected from disclosure to unauthorized persons inside and outside the Company to the same extent as Motorola sensitive, private or confidential information is protected, except where such information was already known to Motorola, is available from other sources, or is generally known outside Motorola or customer organizations.

  Example (a): A customer makes Motorola aware of a confidential project for which he is contemplating use of Motorola products. He asks Motorola to hold the discussion in confidence. His request will be honored. The information will not be disclosed within the Company to persons without a reasonable need to know in order to serve the best interests of that customer. Nor will the information be disclosed to any persons outside the Company except where required to comply with a law or regulation. ("Motorola Code of Conduct")

Choosing Business Partners

- Motorola shall not enter into any agreements with dealers, distributors, agents or consultants . . . which are not in compliance with the applicable laws of the United States and with the laws of any other country that may be involved. . . .

  Example: It would be a violation of this section of the Code to provide a sales agent with a commission on sales of Motorola products which the Motorola employee knows [are] intended to be used in part as a kickback to employees of the customer. ("Motorola Code of Conduct")

- Care must be exercised in selecting those with whom we conduct business. Each business must have processes in place for checking the credit and character of customers and counterparties. These processes must ensure ongoing monitoring of our customers to detect suspicious transactions during the entire period of the relationship. . . . Citicorp does not do business with drug traffickers, money launderers and other criminals. (Citibank, "Code of Conduct and Ethical Policies")

- (See appendix for the Levi Strauss & Co. "Global Sourcing and Operating Guidelines.")

Shareholder Value and Return

- We are committed to providing a superior return to our shareowners, and to protecting and improving the value of their investment through the prudent utilization of corporate resources and by observing the highest standards of legal and ethical conduct in all our business dealings. (United Technologies Corporation, "Corporate Principles")

- We strive to provide a reasonable return to our shareholders and to protect and increase the value of their investment. (AlliedSignal Aerospace, "Code of Conduct")

- Our economic mission is to operate the company on a sound financial basis of profitable growth, increasing value for our shareholders. (Ben &

Jerry's, "Statement of Mission")

- Our final responsibility is to our stockholders. Business must make a sound profit. (Johnson & Johnson, "Our Credo")

Employee Relations

- We believe that people should work because they want or need to, but not because they are forced to do so. We believe that people should work in safe and healthy places that are free from hazardous conditions. We believe people should have access to safe housing, clean water, and health facilities and services.

    We believe that children should not be unlawfully employed as laborers. We believe that if children work, it should not interfere with mandated education.

    We are dedicated to working with others to raise standards of health, education, workplace safety, and economic well-being in all communities where we do business. We believe that wage and benefit levels should address the basic needs of workers and their families. (Starbucks, "Statement of Beliefs")

- We reward people based on relative performance, teamwork and results. (Citibank, "Code of Conduct and Ethical Policies")

- Above all, employees will be provided the same concern, respect and caring attitude within the organization that they are expected to share externally with every Southwest customer. (Southwest Airlines, "Statement of Values")

- Odwalla is a people-centered business. We value responsibility, cooperation and creativity. As a service-oriented company, we are each other's customers, and, as such, it is important that we strive to work together in ways that are mutually satisfying. (Odwalla, "Who Are We and What Are We Doing Here?")

- People have intrinsic worth and dignity. We believe any system or institution that subtracts from that worth and dignity is wrong. Our business experience shows that employees want to work, to contribute, to be a factor in improving things. Few people really wish to be leave the job feeling they haven't made a contribution, or been challenged in some way. . . . [W]e aim to involve employees in improving their own work methods and results, and those of the enterprise as a whole. We intend that participative styles be the cornerstone of our management philosophy. We wish to manage in such a fashion that employees will come to identify in a personal way with the company's economic health. (Caterpillar, "A Code of Worldwide Business Conduct and Operating Principles")

Open Communication Among Staff

- We believe in treating each other with respect and fostering an atmosphere of caring, open communications and candor. (PepsiCo, "Worldwide Code of Conduct")

- Employees must feel free to make suggestions and complaints. (Johnson & Johnson, "Our Credo")

- Each of us must deal openly and honestly with others. Citicorp is committed to discussing job-related concerns in a fair, prompt and impartial manner. (Citibank, "Code of Conduct and Ethical Policies")

- Tell it like it is. Be here now . . . listen and respond with respect. Share ideas and encourage different points of view. Understand the requirement . . . when in doubt ask. (Union Pacific Railroad, "Guidelines on Business Conduct")

- We value Northrop Grumman People . . . We are committed to openness and trust in all relationships. (Northrop Grumman, "Standards of Business Conduct")

Safety

- We are dedicated to designing, constructing, maintaining and operating facilities that protect our people and physical resources. This includes providing and requiring the use of adequate protective equipment and measures and insisting that all work be done safely. (PepsiCo, "Worldwide Code of Conduct")

- Aetna's facilities will be designed and operated in a manner that protects the health and safety of its employees, the public and the environment. . . . Aetna will communicate appropriate safety and health information to employees and the public. ("Aetna Code of Conduct")

- Our attention to safety is based on our full-time commitment to injury-free work, self-worth and a consideration of the well-being of others. Characteristics of Dow Corning raw material, intermediates and products — including toxicity and potential hazards — will be made known to those who produce, package, transport, purchase, use and dispose of them. (Dow Corning, "Code of Conduct")

Personal Growth and Development

- We place a great deal of emphasis on personal integrity and believe long-term results, from real accomplishments, are the only fair way to judge performance.

  We respect the right of individuals to achieve professional and personal balance in their lives. (PepsiCo, "Worldwide Code of Conduct")

- We must be mindful of ways to help our employees fulfill their family responsibilities. (Johnson & Johnson, "Our Credo")

- Be a well-regarded employer that is mindful of the well-being of our people, allowing them to develop their individual capabilities in an impartial environment and offering them the opportunity for career advancement. ("United Parcel Service Mission Statement")

- We treat one another with respect and take pride in the significant contributions that come from the diversity of individuals and ideas. Our continued success requires us to provide the education and development needed to help our people grow. (Northrop Grumman, "Standards of Business Conduct")

Diversity

- Aetna's Equal Opportunity program provides that all Company programs and benefits are to be administered without discrimination based on race, color, sex, national origin, religion, age, disability, veteran status, sexual orientation or marital status. . . .

  Any request, irrespective of its source, to reassign an employee on the basis of race, sex, religion, age, disability or other inappropriate criteria will not be honored. We will not compromise our right to make assignments free from these considerations, even if faced with the loss of business.

Slurs, epithets, jokes, or any other harassing actions, based on race, color, sex, national origin, religion, age, disability, veteran status, sexual orientation or marital status are prohibited. ("Aetna Code of Conduct")

- There must be equal opportunity for employment, development and advancement for those qualified. (Johnson & Johnson, "Our Credo")

- We believe that diversity in our staff is important to our success as a global organization. . . . Discrimination of any kind is counterproductive to our performance. (Citibank, "Code of Conduct and Ethical Policies")

Pursuit of Excellence

- Our mission is to be the leader of our industry, and that calls for excellence in every part of the business by each employee. We must pursue excellence in the quality of each product, service, and contact. We debate the issues, but once a decision is made, commitment is expected from everyone. Our success depends upon the achievement of excellence through teamwork. Our integrity, as a company and as individuals, must always be without question. Through excellence, we will meet and exceed the expectations of others. (Coca-Cola, "Code of Business Conduct: Our Values")

- We must experiment with new ideas. Research must be carried on, innovative programs developed and mistakes paid for. New equipment must be purchased, new facilities provided and new products launched. Reserves must be created to provide for adverse times. (Johnson & Johnson, "Our Credo")

Relationship to the Political Process

- No funds or assets of the Company shall be used for federal, state or local political campaign contributions. These prohibitions cover not only direct contributions but also indirect assistance or support of candidates or political parties through purchase of tickets to special dinners or other fundraising events or the furnishing of any other goods, services or equipment to political parties or committees.

No funds or assets of the Company shall be used directly or indirectly for political contributions outside the United States, even where permitted by applicable law, without the prior written approval of the Chief Executive Officer or General Counsel.

The above prohibitions apply only to the direct or indirect use of corporate funds or assets for political purposes and are, of course, not intended to discourage employees from making personal contributions to the candidates, parties or committees of their choice, through the Company's Political Action Committee. Under no circumstances shall employees be reimbursed in any way for personal contributions. (Provident Mutual, "Code of Conduct")

- Nortel does not abuse corporate power to influence public issues — nor does it become involved in unethical political activity. It does, however, express its views on local and national issues which affect its operations. The corporation respects and supports the right of all employees to participate in the political process. However, it does not reimburse employees for personal political contributions, nor does it permit employees to campaign on company time or property. (Northern Telecom, "Code of Business Conduct")

Suppliers and Distributors

- PepsiCo will . . . make clear to all suppliers that we expect them to compete fairly and vigorously for our business, and we will select our suppliers strictly on merit. (PepsiCo, "Worldwide Code of Conduct")

- Our suppliers and distributors must have an opportunity to make a fair profit. (Johnson & Johnson, "Our Credo")

- We owe our suppliers the same type of respect that we show to our customers. Our suppliers deserve fair and equitable treatment, clear agreements and honest feedback on performance. We consider our suppliers' needs in conducting all aspects of our business. ("Northrop Grumman Values")

Competitor Relations

- Nortel employees do not denigrate competitors and their products, but do, with care and prudence, make fair and factually-based comparisons on attributes such as price and performance. They do not improperly seek competitors' information. (Northern Telecom, "Code of Business Conduct")

- PepsiCo will . . . compete vigorously and with integrity; never criticize a competitor's product without a good basis for such statements, or act in a manner designed to exclude competitors from the workplace. (PepsiCo, "Worldwide Code of Conduct")

- It has long been IBM's policy to sell products and services on their merits, not by disparaging competitors, their products or their services. False or misleading statements and innuendos are improper. Don't make comparisons that unfairly cast the competitor in a bad light. Such conduct only invites disrespect from customers and complaints from competitors.

  In short, stress the advantages of IBM products and services, and be sure that all comparisons are fair and accurate. (International Business Machines, "Business Conduct Guidelines)

Antitrust Provisions

- Citicorp's strategies and other decisions must be made independently without consultation with Citicorp's competitors. . . . Except for bona-fide loan syndications or other legitimate associations permitted by law, Citicorp employees should not discuss or enter into arrangements with competitors. (Citibank, "Code of Conduct and Ethical Policies")

- We will compete vigorously in each of our industries while maintaining a strict regard for compliance in all respects with the anti-trust laws. (Vulcan Materials, "Mission Statement")

Environment

- We believe in the importance of progressive environmental practices and conservation efforts. We believe in demonstrating leadership for environmental practices in countries in which we do business. We believe that hazardous materials such as chemicals and pesticides should be used safely and responsibly, if at all. (Starbucks, "Statement of Beliefs")

- We are committed to minimizing the impact of our businesses on the environment with methods that are socially responsible, scientifically based and economically sound. We encourage conservation, recycling and energy use programs that promote clean air and water and reduce landfill waste. (PepsiCo, "Worldwide Code of Conduct")

- We must maintain in good order the property we are privileged to use, protecting the environment and natural resources. (Johnson & Johnson, "Our Credo")

- Aetna will promote, to the maximum extent feasible, the recycling, recovery and reuse of residual materials resulting from our business operations. . . . Aetna will continue to encourage employees to use van/car pools and public transportation. ("Aetna Code of Conduct")

- Environmental, health and safety risk assessments shall be conducted as early as possible in the development and planning stage of process design, facility design, acquisitions and divestitures. Periodic assessments of the environmental, health and safety status of each facility must be performed. Pollution prevention will be achieved by eliminating or minimizing waste generation at the source and, if necessary, controlling the pollutant. (Honeywell, "Code of Ethics and Business Conduct")

Responsibility to the Community

- We are responsible to the communities in which we live and work and to the world community as well. We must be good citizens — support good works and charities and bear our fair share of taxes. We must encourage civic improvements and better health and education. (Johnson & Johnson, "Our Credo")

International Operations

- We obey all laws and regulations and respect the lawful customs of host countries. We recognize and pay particular attention to each country's priorities regarding economic and social development, including industrial and regional growth, environmental quality, employment and training opportunities, and the transfer and advancement of technology and innovation. (PepsiCo, "Worldwide Code of Conduct")

- It is Honeywell's policy to comply with U.S. antiboycott legislation, which is intended to prevent Honeywell from taking any action in support of a boycott imposed by a foreign country upon a country which is friendly to the United States. All employees are responsible for advising the Office of General Counsel of any boycott-related occurrence, development or investigation of possible legal significance to the company. The receipt of a boycott request must be reported immediately whether or not the transaction takes place. (Honeywell, "Code of Ethics and Business Conduct")

- (See appendix for the Levi Strauss "Global Sourcing and Operating Guidelines.")

Labor Conditions, Child Labor

- The factory does not use involuntary labor of any kind, including prison labor, debt bondage or forced labor by governments.

  Factories shall employ only workers who meet the applicable minimum legal age requirement or are at least 14 years of age, whichever is greater.

  Factories shall not use corporal punishment or any other form of physical or psychological coercion. Factories must be sufficiently lighted and ventilated, aisles accessible, machinery maintained, and hazardous materials sensibly stored and disposed of. Factories providing housing for their workers must keep these facilities clean and safe. . . .

  Workers are paid at least the minimum legal wage or the local industry standard, whichever is greater. The factory does not require, on a regularly scheduled basis, a work week in excess of 60 hours. Workers may refuse overtime without any threat of penalty, punishment or dismissal. Workers have at least one day off in seven. (Gap, Inc., "Code of Vendor Conduct")

Accounting, Self-Reporting

- Accuracy and reliability in the preparation of all business records is mandated by law. It is of critical importance to the corporate decision-making process and to the proper discharge of Provident Mutual's financial, legal and reporting obligations. All business records, expense accounts, vouchers, bills, payroll and service records and other reports are to be prepared with care and honesty. False or misleading entries are not permitted in the books and records of Provident Mutual or Any affiliated company. All corporate funds and assets are to be recorded in accordance with applicable corporate procedures. Compliance with accounting procedures is required at all times. It is the responsibility of all employees to insure that both the letter and the spirit of corporate accounting and internal control procedures are strictly adhered to at all times. They should advise the responsible person in their department of any shortcomings they observe in such procedures.

- All business records, expense accounts, vouchers, bills, payrolls, service records, reports to government agencies, and other reports, books and records of the Company must be prepared with care and honesty. . . . Time slips and time cards must be completed accurately and promptly. All employees must report only the time and actual number of hours they have worked. Reporting of hours not actually worked, but for which an employee is entitled to be paid under a labor contract, must also be true and accurate. (Union Pacific, "Guidelines on Business Conduct")

- Appropriate records must be kept of all transactions. Employees are expected to cooperate fully with our internal and external auditors. Information must not be falsified or concealed under any circumstance and an employee whose activities cause false financial reporting will be subject to disciplinary action including discharge. (PepsiCo, "Worldwide Code of Conduct")

- Financial information provided to Citicorp's shareholders, regulatory bodies and others requires the highest standards of fairness and accuracy. Making false or misleading statements to anyone including internal or external auditors, Citicorp counsel, other Citicorp employees or regulators is prohibited and constitutes a falsification of records. (Citibank, "Code of Conduct and Ethical Policies")

Disclosure

- An employee or another agent, authorized to act on behalf of Citicorp, who suspects a possible violation of a law, regulation, or Citicorp ethical standard should report the suspected violation to his or her supervisor promptly. . . .

The following categories of actual and potential losses arising out of forgery, fraud and operating errors must be reported to the Corporate Audit Investigations & Potential Loss Unit:

1. Any actual or potential loss of the equivalent of US $25,000 or more;

2. Any mysterious disappearance of the equivalent of US $1,000 or more;

3. Any incident involving actual or suspected financial wrongdoing — regardless of amount.

4. Any employee wrongdoing, regardless of amount involved.

(Citibank, "Code of Conduct and Ethical Policies")

- Every employee shall disclose promptly to his or her immediate supervisor any personal situation or transaction which is or may be in conflict with the intent or spirit of this Code. The supervisor shall determine what action should be taken and recommend that action in writing for approval by the next higher level of management. (PepsiCo, "Worldwide Code of Conduct")

- Discipline may be taken against an employee who has deliberately failed to report a violation or deliberately withheld information concerning a violation of the Honeywell Code of Ethics and Business Conduct. (Honeywell, "Code of Ethics and Business Conduct")

Whistleblowing

- No employee who reports a suspected violation of law, regulation or Corporate policy will be retaliated against as a result of having made the report. (Citibank, "Code of Conduct and Ethical Policies")

- The Company will make every effort to ensure that no retribution of any kind will be taken against any uninvolved person for reporting evidence of fraud, dishonesty, criminal conduct or any other activity prohibited by the Company. ("Aetna Code of Conduct")

- It is a violation of Union Pacific's policies and these guidelines to discriminate or retaliate against an employee for reporting information to the Director of Ethics and Compliance . . . No employee will be disciplined or harassed in any way for making honest reports of violations. ("Union Pacific Guidelines on Business Conduct")

Conflicts of Interest, Inside Information

- PepsiCo's conflicts of interest policy is straightforward: Don't compete with PepsiCo businesses, and never let your business dealings on behalf of any of our businesses be influenced, or appear to be influenced, by personal or family interests. Examples of conflicts that must be disclosed and resolved include:

  1. Having a family interest in a transaction with PepsiCo or one of its divisions or subsidiaries (the Company).

  2. Having a substantial interest in a competitor, supplier or customer of the Company.

3. Having a substantial interest in an organization that has, or seeks to do business with, the Company.

4. Participating in a venture where the Company has expressed an interest.

5. Acquiring an interest in property (such as real estate, patent rights, securities or other properties) where the Company has, or might have, an interest.

6. Receiving a gift, favor, loan, special service, payment or special treatment of any kind from any individual or organization which conducts or seeks to conduct business with the Company, or which competes with the Company, unless:

   a. It would be consistent with good business practices.

   b. It could not be construed as a business inducement.

   c. It is of nominal value.

   d. Public disclosure of the transaction would not embarrass PepsiCo.

   (PepsiCo "Worldwide Code of Conduct")

- We must avoid circumstances in which our personal interests conflict, or may appear to conflict, with the interests of Citicorp or its customers. Situations that may lead to actual or apparent conflict include (but are not limited to):

   - Participating in decisions to do business with organizations in which you or a close family member has an interest or from which personal benefit may accrue.

   - Business done with Citicorp only through friendship, family ties, giving or receiving gifts, or to gain favor.

   - Misuse of Citicorp's name for personal benefit.

   - Citicorp employees may invest for their own personal account as long as those investments do not involve a conflict of interest with the activities of Citicorp or its customers. Employee investment decisions must be based solely on publicly available information.

   Citicorp employees are discouraged from serving as directors, trustees, officers or advisors for outside for-profit organizations except in very special circumstances. Prior approval from the Committee on Good Corporate Practice is required before you may accept a directorship or secondary employment. It must not pose a conflict or the appearance of a conflict with the interests of Citicorp, nor interfere with your ability to perform your Citicorp responsibilities, and not have an adverse impact on the business interests of the Corporation. (Citibank, "Code of Conduct and Ethical Policies")

- Employees should not permit personal interest to conflict, or even to appear to conflict, with their Aetna duties. In particular:

  ◆ No employee may benefit personally from Aetna's dealings with others.

  ◆ No employee may serve interests that compete with Aetna's.

  ◆ No outside activities may interfere with Aetna job performance.

  If you plan to take a position of responsibility or acquire a significant ownership interest in a business outside Aetna, you must report your intentions on the compliance form before you enter into the relationship. . . . You should discuss the relationship with your Compliance Officer even before reporting it. If you already have such a relationship, report it immediately.

  ("Aetna Code of Conduct")

- Our policies . . . require every Union Pacific employee to avoid any relationship with persons or firms with whom Union Pacific transacts, or is likely to transact, business which may place employees in a conflict of interest situation to the possible detriment of themselves and Union Pacific. (Union Pacific Guidelines on Business Conduct)

- A former employee, other than a retired or laid-off employee, who, after the termination of his or her active employment with Honeywell, establishes his or her business, may not be a supplier or consultant to Honeywell for two years from such termination except as specifically authorized in writing by the business unit vice president. Except as authorized by the cognizant location manager or vice president, purchases may not be made for two years through a former Honeywell employee (except a retired or laid-off employee) who is representing a vendor and who at any time in the previous two years had responsibility for or influenced procurement at Honeywell in the operation which he or she is seeking to solicit. (Honeywell, "Code of Ethics and Business Conduct")

Insider Trading

- Employees should not effect any transaction in the securities of PepsiCo or another company involved with PepsiCo while they have material nonpublic information about that Company. Employees should not disclose material nonpublic information to anyone outside PepsiCo (including family members), except where disclosure is needed to enable PepsiCo to carry on its business, and where there is no reason to believe-because of an agreement or otherwise-that the information will be misused or improperly disclosed by the recipient. (PepsiCo, "Worldwide Code of Conduct")

- Citicorp policy strictly prohibits any officer or employee of Citicorp, whenever and in whatever capacity employed, from trading for his or her own account, or for the profit of family members or friends, on the basis of inside information. (Citibank, "Code of Conduct and Ethical Policies")

- All employees are forbidden from trading securities while in possession of material nonpublic information or disclosing such information to others (I) inside the Company except for business purposes or (II) outside the Company except with the approval of Law and Regulatory Affairs. ("Aetna Code of Conduct")

- Any employee who is aware of material information related to Honeywell or to firms with which Honeywell is negotiating or competing may not buy or sell shares or other securities of Honeywell or these firms or disclose this information to any other person outside the company until the information has been disclosed to the public and has had an adequate opportunity to be absorbed by the market. (Honeywell, "Code of Ethics and Business Conduct")

In an article for *Fortune*, Thomas A. Stewart takes a swipe at vision statements whipped up in standard, meaningless corporatespeak. Companies with integrity-deficit disorder might try his "Handy-Dandy Vision Crafter":

Select one to three items from each group below, add your logo, marinate overnight in Scotch and red wine, and serve with a straight face.

Our Vision

To be a . . .

A) *premier; leading;*
preeminent; world-class; growing

company that provides . . .

B) *innovative; cost-effective;*
focused; diversified; high-quality
C) *products; services; products and services*

to . . .

D) *serve the global marketplace;*
create shareholder value; fulfill our covenants
with our stakeholders; delight our customers

in the rapidly changing . . .

E) *information-solutions; business-solutions;*
consumer-solutions; financial-solutions

industries.

From Thomas A. Stewart's "A Refreshing Change: Vision Statements That Make Sense," *Fortune*, Sept. 30, 1996

Resources on Ethics Codes

Websites

- **Center for the Study of Ethics in the Professions – Codes of Ethics Online**
  http://ethics.iit.edu/codes
  A vast library of ethics codes.

- **Ethics Resource Center – Ethics Resources**
  www.ethics.org/resources
  Includes articles, books and links on ethics codes.

- **Ethicsweb.ca**
  www.ethicsweb.ca/codes
  Created by a professor at Saint Mary's University in Halifax, Canada, this site includes information and resources on ethics codes.

- **Institute of Business Ethics – Codes of Conduct**
  www.ibe.org.uk/codesofconduct.html
  An extensive section on ethics codes.

- **Web-miner.com – Business Ethics Codes**
  www.web-miner.com/busethics.htm#codes
  Includes links to over two dozen companies' codes of conduct.

Books and Articles

American Academy of Ophthalmology. "Ethics in Ophthalmology: A Practical Guide," 1996.

Baker, L. W. *The Credibility Factor*. Homewood, IL: Business One Irwin, 1993.

Barnaby J. F. "Helping Corporate America Hew to the Straight and Narrow," *The New York Times*, November 3, 1991, p. F5.

Barth, S.R., Foley Steven, Lardner Steven and Aspatore Books Staff. *Corporate Ethics: How to Update or Develop Your Ethics Code so That it Is in Compliance With the New Laws of Corporate Responsibility*, Boston: Aspatore Books, 2003.

Benson, G. "Codes of Ethics," *Journal of Business Ethics*, 8, 1989, pp. 302-319.

Berenbeim, R. *Corporate Ethics*, New York: The Conference Board, 1987.

Berenbeim, R. *Corporate Ethics Practices*. New York: The Conference Board, 1992.

The Business Roundtable. *Corporate Ethics: A Prime Business Asset*, New York, 1988.

Collins, J.C. and J.I. Porras. "Building Your Company's Vision," *Harvard Business Review* (Sept./Oct. 1996), pp. 65-77.

Caroselli, M. *The Business Ethics Activity Book: 50 Exercises for Promoting Integrity at Work*, New York: AMACOM, 2003

The Conference Board. *Corporate Ethics: Developing New Standards of Accountability*, New York, 1991.

Del Vecchio, G. and R. Fong. *A Knight's Code of Business: How to Achieve Character and Competence in the Corporate World*, Ithaca, NY: Paramount Market Pub., 2003.

Driscoll, D. M., W. M. Hoffman and E. S. Petry. *The Ethical Edge*, New York: MasterMedia, 1995.

Drucker, P. "What Is Business Ethics?" *The Public Interest*, Spring 1981.

Ethics Resource Center. *Creating a Workable Company Code of Ethics*, Washington, DC: Ethics Resource Center, 2003.

Ethics Resource Center. *Ethics Policies and Programs in American Business*, Washington DC: Ethics Resource Center, 1990.

Farnham, A. "State Your Values, Hold the Hot Air," *Fortune*, April 19, 1993.

Frankel, M. S. "Professional Codes: Why, How and with What Impact?" *Journal of Business Ethics* 8, 1989, pp. 109-115.

Fromson, B. D. "Mutual Mystery: Funds' Codes of Conduct," *Washington Post*, June 30, 1996, p. H1.

Gorlin, R. A. *Codes of Professional Responsibility* (3rd ed.). Washington, DC: The Bureau of National Affairs, 1986, 1990, 1994.

Lefebvre, M. and Singh, J. B. "The Content and Focus of Canadian Corporate Codes of Ethics," *Journal of Business Ethics*, October 1992.

Manley, W. W. *Executive's Handbook of Model Business Conduct Codes*, Englewood Cliffs, NJ: Prentice-Hall, 1991.

Murphy, P.E. (ed.). *Eighty Exemplary Ethics Statements*, Notre Dame, IN: University of Notre Dame Press, 1997.

Newton, L. H. and M. M. Ford (eds.). *Taking Sides: Clashing Views on Controversial Issues in Business Ethics and Society* (4th ed.). Guilford, CT: Dushkin, 1996.

Seglin, J.L. and Norman R. Augustine. *The Good, the Bad, and Your Business: Choosing Right When Ethical Dilemmas Pull You Apart,* 2000.

Stewart, T. A. "A Refreshing Change: Vision Statements That Make Sense," *Fortune*, September 30, 1996.

Touche Ross. *Ethics In American Business: A Special Report*. New York: Touche Ross, 1988.

Weaver, G. R. "Does Ethics Code Design Matter? Effects of Ethics Code Rationales and Sanctions on Recipients' Justice Perceptions and Content Recall," *Journal of Business Ethics,* 14, 1995, pp. 367-385.

Williams, O. (ed). *Global Codes of Conduct: An Idea Whose Time Has Come* (The John W. Houck Notre Dame Series in Business Ethics), Notre Dame, IN: University of Notre Dame Press, 2000.

We encourage readers to share their own best practices for inclusion in future editions of this book. Send your correspondence via e-mail or regular mail, and visit the Institute online.

Josephson Institute of Ethics
Dept. of Publications and Communications
9841 Airport Blvd., Suite 300, Los Angeles, CA 90045
www.josephsoninstitute.org; www.charactercounts.org
(310) 846-4800 or (800) 711-2670

More resources from the Josephson Institute of Ethics

The Josephson Institute of Ethics is active in all aspects of ethics education, from youth, through its CHARACTER COUNTS! initiative, to adults, through its *Ethics and Effectiveness in the Workplace* training seminars and consulting services. The Institute has also partnered with leaders in adult ethics education, from the Society for Human Resource Management to the Ethics Officer Association and the Better Business Bureau.

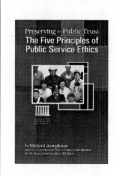

Preserving the Public Trust
The Five Principles of
Public Service Ethics

This book brings to life the Josephson Institute's five principles of public service ethics: public interest, independent objective judgment, public accountability, democratic leadership, and responsibility and fitness for office. It includes extensive references to the Office of Government Ethics rules for federal employees.

(6" x 9", softcover, 140 pages)
Item #50-0870
$13.99

Making Ethical Decisions

Moral questions can be knotty. This comprehensive primer examines the hows and whys of making choices that withstand ethical scrutiny. With realistic examples and a step-by-step decision-making model, this easy-to-read booklet is ideal for the individual reader — or as a training guide for any organization that wishes to help its employees find the way through difficult issues to successful choices.

(5.5" x 8.5", softcover, 33 pages)
Item #50-0450
$7.95

Commentaries
by Michael Josephson

Every day, listeners around the world tune in to hear Michael Josephson's take on the issues that define our days and lives. From business and world affairs to sports and parenting, Mr. Josephson offers the unique perspective of one of the country's best-known ethicists and most innovative teachers. Now his favorite commentaries — featuring the humor, compassion and tough talk he is renowned for — are available in these hardcover gift volumes and in a two-CD set.

(Books are 5" x 7", hardcover with dust jacket)

You Don't Have to Be Sick to Get Better!	**Item #50-5000**	**$20.00**
The Best Is Yet to Come	**Item #50-5010**	**$20.00**
Both books	**Item #50-5020sp**	**$35.00**
Making Your Character Count double CD	**Item #05-1190**	**$20.00**

Order by calling (800) 711-2670 or online at: www.charactercounts.org

Printed in the United States
123333LV00003B/3/A